AF291445

ENVELOPE ART

A Selection from the
W H Chignell collection

Published in 2026 by Unicorn
an imprint of Unicorn Publishing Group
Charleston Studio
Meadow Business Centre
Lewes BN8 5RW
www.unicornpublishing.org

ISBN 978-1-918271-02-7
10 9 8 7 6 5 4 3 2 1

Designed by Karen Wilks
Printed in Serbia by Publikum

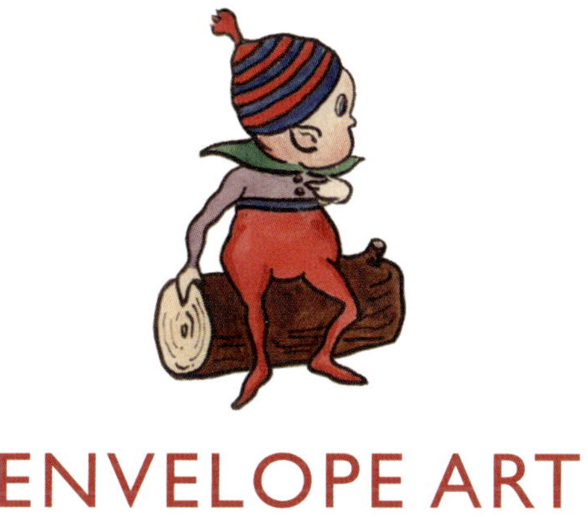

ENVELOPE ART

A Selection from the
W H Chignell collection

Chosen by James P Carley and
the layout organised by Katharine E Hutchison

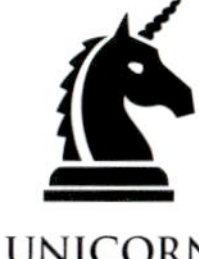

UNICORN

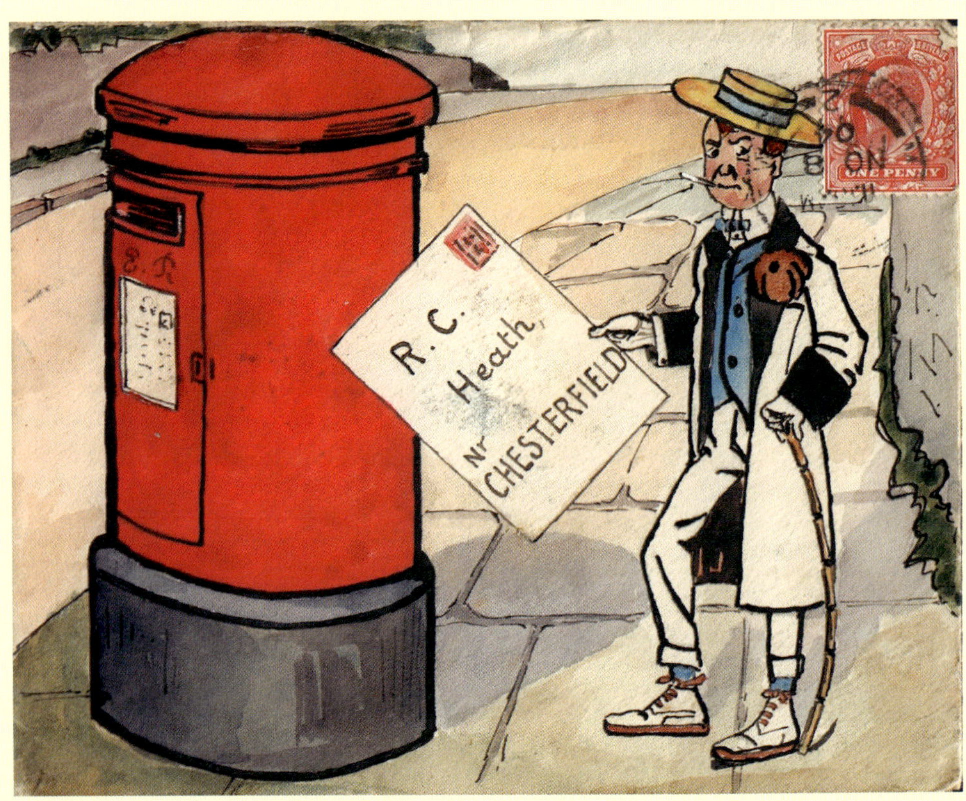

R. C. Heath, Nr CHESTERFIELD
ONE PENNY

Foreword

In 1840 THE WAY PEOPLE COMMUNICATED IN BRITAIN, and indeed
throughout the world, changed. Uniform Penny Postage
revolutionised the way people stayed in touch and opened the
postal service to millions of people.

For hundreds of years people have communicated over distance
in writing. Sending messages home from far flung parts of the
world, undertaking political discussions or transacting business.
For most of this history however, letter writing and the ability to
stay in touch was limited by two factors, being able to read and
write, and the ability to pay the cost of sending a letter.

In Britain cost had been a major obstacle since the postal service
opened to public use under King Charles I in 1635. Charles
allowed the public to use his personal mail service, his Royal
Mail, for the first time. His motivation was money, to bring in
revenue to support his lifestyle but by bypassing the need to go
to his parliament for funds. The postal service was complicated
and expensive. Letters were charged for based on distance rather
than size, the further the letter travelled the more expensive it
was. Additional sheets of paper were also charged for, the more

you wrote the more it cost. This resulted in people being very
aware of how they used the post. It was limited in its use, only
the key bits of information were included to keep the cost down.
Letters were folded and sealed, usually with wax – no envelopes.
That would just have increased the cost for no benefit.

The most direct consequence of this was that only the wealthier
in society could afford to use the postal service. Letters could
cost more than a week's wage for an average labourer, so well out
of reach for many people.

But in the 1830s Britain was undergoing reforms, political
equality was being explored, although it was almost a 100
years later before this was truly achieved. Social reforms were
happening, and the working conditions of society were slowly
being improved, or at the very least considered.

Education for the working classes was being considered by
some, and school teacher Rowland Hill, felt that if the postal
service was more affordable then perhaps working people might
be more inclined to want to learn to read and write. He worked

with other social reformers petitioning the government to reform the postal service.

The result of this was the 1840 Uniform Penny Postage. The notion that you could send a letter, under half an ounce in weight, to any part of Britain for One Penny. Suddenly the cost barrier had gone. The post office was initially cautious that this huge cost reduction would impact their ability to carry out the logistics of transporting the mail. However, very quickly it became apparent that the great increase in the use of the post meant that it was making more money from the service, not less.

This also meant that now more or less anyone could afford to send a letter. Additionally, the removal of the distance charge and the number of sheets of paper restriction, meant people could now enclose their letters in envelopes. At the Great Exhibition of 1851 an envelope making machine was among the exhibits showcased. Suddenly the postal service was undergoing significant change.

Before 1840, letters were paid for by the recipient, as they had to make the journey before the distance could be determined, and thus the cost. With a flat fee for postage, payment could take place in advance, with the sender paying the cost. Pre-payment was via the purchase of a postage stamp and on 6th May 1840 the world's first postage stamp became valid for use. The Penny Black was introduced, a small black stamp bearing the image of a young Queen Victoria.

The basic design of the standard postage stamp has remained largely unaltered since that first stamp in 1840. For the first time miniature works of art started to appear on letters.

Soon after the reform of the postal service people started to personalise letters, initially by using the stamp to send secret messages in something that became known as the language of stamps. Placing stamps at angles to convey sentiments such as 'Forget me not', 'I love you' and 'In thoughts with you'. Around a similar time, creative Victorians also began to illustrate envelopes, either decoratively or in a coded fashion. A trend for a while was to encode messages or puzzles for the postal workers, creating cryptic addresses. The post had now become a source of fun, social interaction and entertainment. Something the reforms of the 1840s allowed for the first time.

This fashion for mail art became more known in the 1950s when artist Ray Johnson started using the post to send artworks to friends and colleagues. The post became not just a means to send art but part of the artform itself. Being used both as part of the work, with modern artists such as Peter Liversage creating works that travel though the post, as well as a canvas for art though the illustrated envelope.

The largest collection of mail art in The Postal Museum's collection is that created by Frederick Charles Tolhurst, for which the Museum holds over 100 examples. Tolhurst created some elaborate illustrated envelopes sent to his family, and most especially his daughter Vera between 1909 and 1934. The Museum's collection also holds similar mail art created by artist Jacqui McLennan who not only created works herself in the mid 1970s, but sent blank envelopes and stamps to friends and fellow artists asking them to create their own works and send them back. The post was the focus of the art and moved from being a canvas for some fun family creations to being part of the art in itself.

The work of William Henry Chignell spans a similar period to that of Tolhurst, and they share something of a style and motivation in their work, both creating art on envelopes for the benefit of family. This publication is a beautiful celebration of the art of the envelope, the love of family and a snap shot into the social impact of the post. A platform for art and communication.

It is testament to the importance and role of the postal service which touches people's lives. An example of why physical, tangible post is so important throughout history, a way to stay in touch but also how to bring fun, care and creativity to the act of sending a letter.

Chris Taft
Head of Collections
The Postal Museum

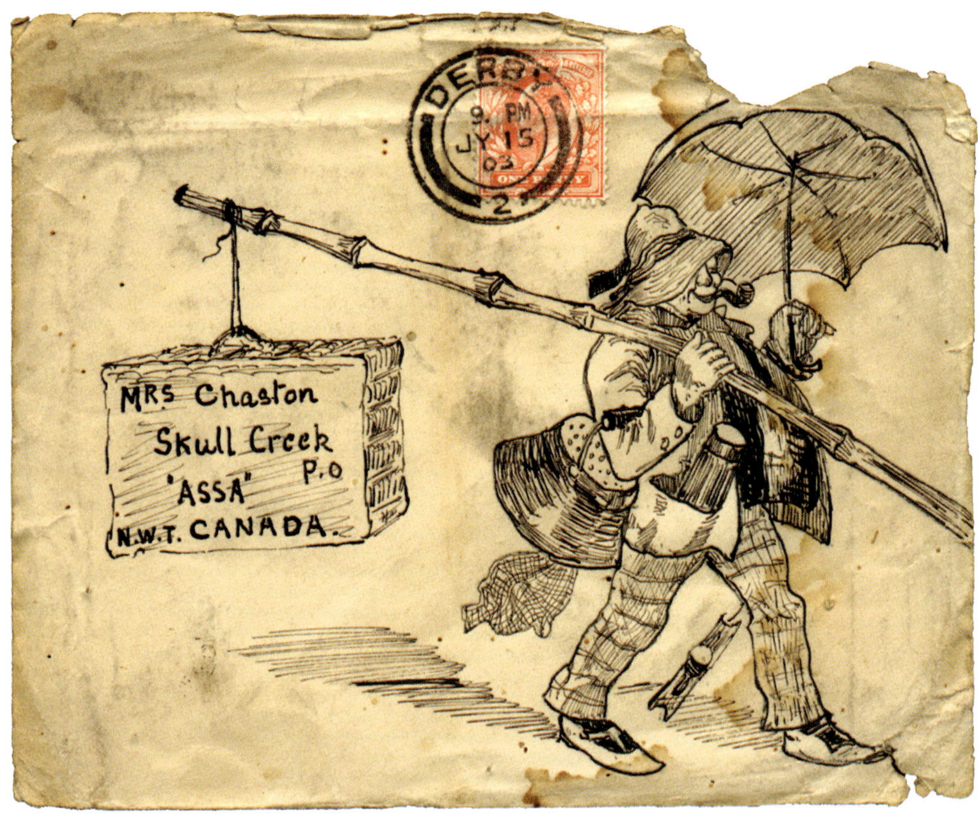
MRs Chaston
Skull Creek
'ASSA'   P.O
N.W.T. CANADA.

Introduction

DURING THEIR LIFETIMES, for William Henry Chignell (1841–1933) and Eliza Leys Chignell (1844–1914), the only way to communicate at a distance was by letter or telegram. Their own parents travelled extensively and their children in turn became intrepid travellers. Typical of families of their class and education they were closely knit and letters were crucial to them; the siblings wrote regularly to their parents and to one another.

Letters themselves lost or destroyed, what does survive are a large number of envelopes. Each had a water-colour drawing on the front and often the address was incorporated into the design. The drawings show extraordinary talent and range: from ironic sketches, to witty commentary, and to beautiful scenes. As active as the children were as writers, no surviving document describes their reactions to the envelopes. Our only knowledge of how they must have been treasured lies in the fact they were not destroyed.

In this book we have attempted to provide indications of where the children would have been when they received the envelopes and what they must have meant to them and to the communities in which they were living. It seems to us that understanding the designs in their wider context brings them to life in ways that the envelopes on their own, attractive as they are, cannot do.

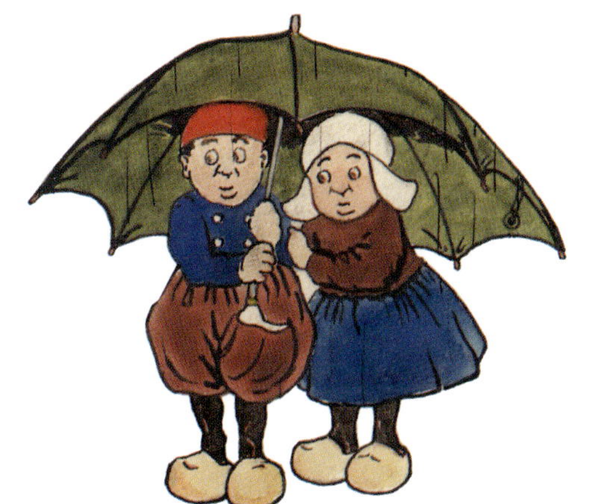

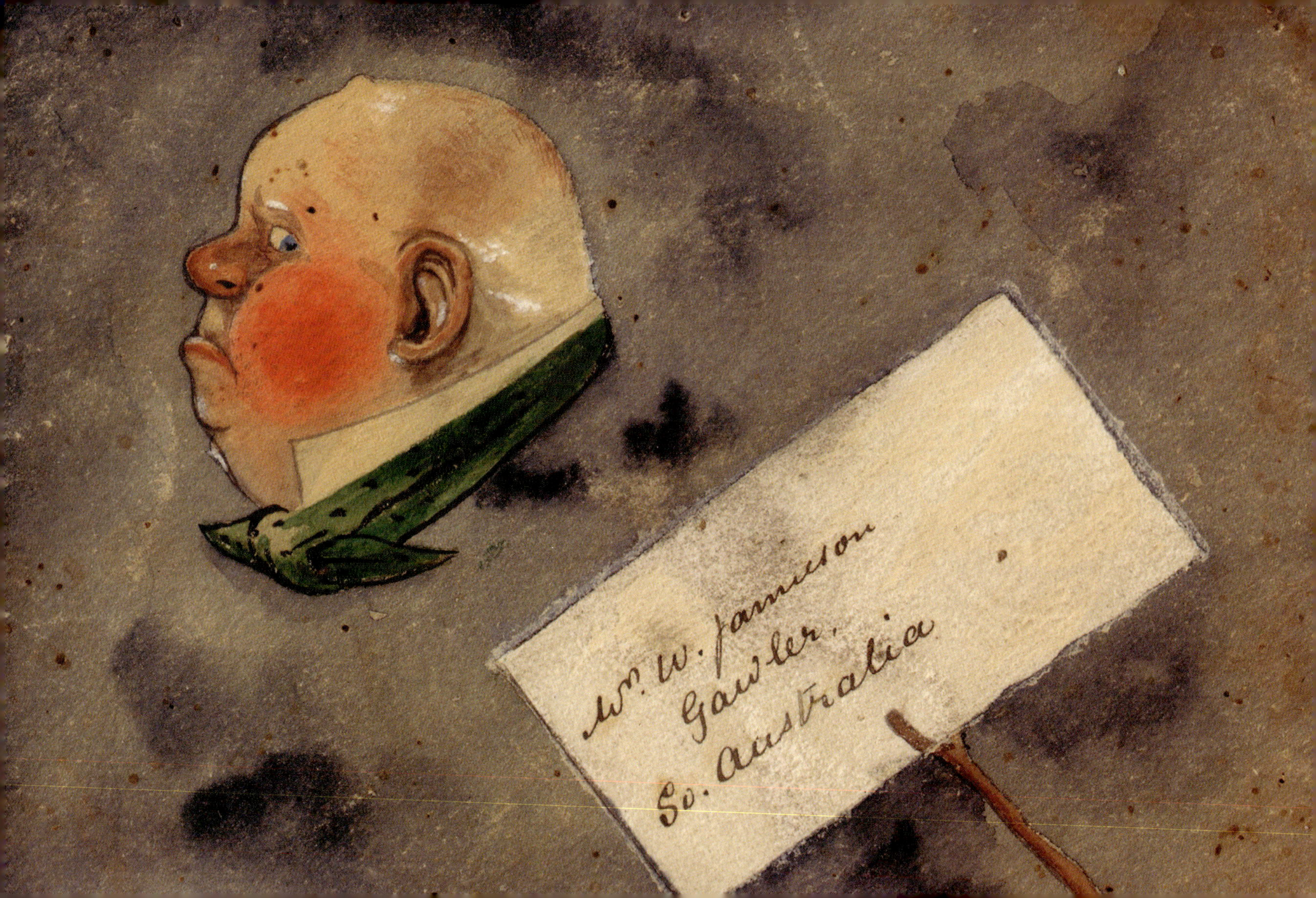

Mr W. Jamison
Gawler.
So. Australia

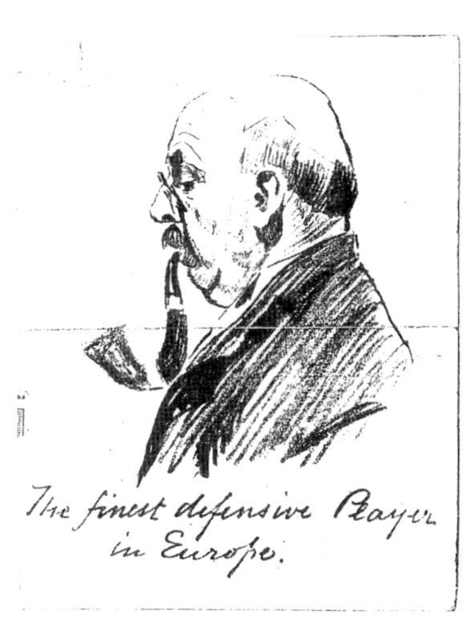

ALTHOUGH a member of a hardworking and talented family who were involved in education and the arts, William Henry Chignell never achieved his potential. His only legacy consists of the hand-painted envelopes, most dashed off in commercial hotels and sent to amuse his children scattered around Britain and in far-flung corners of the Empire. Talent he had, but he lacked perseverence and dedication: it is only by chance that so many of his charming paintings in such an unexpected medium are still intact.

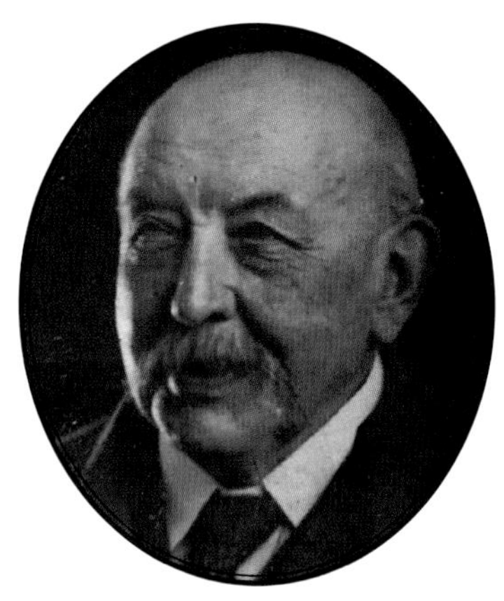

HARRY, AS HE WAS CALLED, was born on 30 March 1841 in Ampthill, Bedfordshire. He came from a long line of Dissenters who had lived in Colchester from at least the seventeenth century. His cousin William Hale White, a.k.a. Mark Rutherford, the social reformer and novelist, gives a description in his *Early Life* of their mutual grandmother, Mary Ann Hale, one that evokes the world from which Harry sprang and the household which he too would have visited as a small boy and where, perhaps, he got his first taste for music, his love of gardens, and his fascination with those on the fringes of society:

My maternal grandmother was a little, round, old lady, with a ruddy, healthy tinge on her face. She lived in Queen Street [in Colchester] in a house dated 1619 over the doorway. There was a pleasant garden at the back, and the scent of a privet hedge in it has never to this day left me. In one of the rooms was a spinet. The strings were struck with quills, and gave a thin, twangling, or rather twingling sound. In that house I was taught by a stupid servant to be frightened by gipsies. She threatened me with them after I was in bed.

As well as more commendable traits, Harry may also have acquired from his grandmother a taste for fine living that would be his downfall more than once: she was the sister of a wealthy silk manufacturer and a putative descendant of the influential jurist Sir Matthew Hale.

Harry's father William (1811-1884) left Colchester as a young man and moved first to Ampthill and then to Romsey where, like Rutherford's father would do in Bedford, he established himself as a printer, bookseller and publisher. After William's death his wife Mary (1813–1890) carried on the business and she in turn was succeeded by Harry's sister Mary Elizabeth (d. 1913): his children, the later recipients of his letters and envelopes, would later stay with their grandmother and aunt during summer holidays.

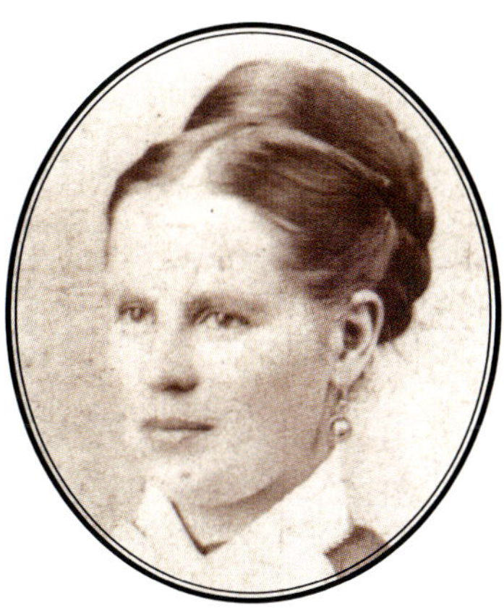

Unlike his siblings, Harry, who was artistic and a dreamer rather than a businessman, left Romsey and struck out on his own. His future wife, Eliza Leys, was the daughter of James Leys, Chief Engineer on HMS *Achilles*. Eliza had been a boarder at Harrage Hall in Romsey. Several years later Eliza's younger sister Jemima attended the school where her closest friend was Mary Elizabeth Chignell whose brother Harry would marry Eliza after the death of their father in 1865 who had left his entire estate to his 'lawfully begotten' daughters Eliza and Jemima.

By this time, some twenty-four years old and already a widower, Harry was described as a professor of music. Where he had been trained is not clear, but musical talent ran in the family. His nephew Robert Chignell, for example, would later come to prominence as a composer of opera and orchestral works, including the music for a BBC adaptation of *Les Misérables*.

Harry and Eliza were married in 1867. Following a honeymoon in Paris they settled in Leighton Buzzard where three children were born and Harry was organist and choir master at All Saints' Church, Eliza a soloist in the choir. Theirs gave the appearance of a happy collaboration and a settled life.

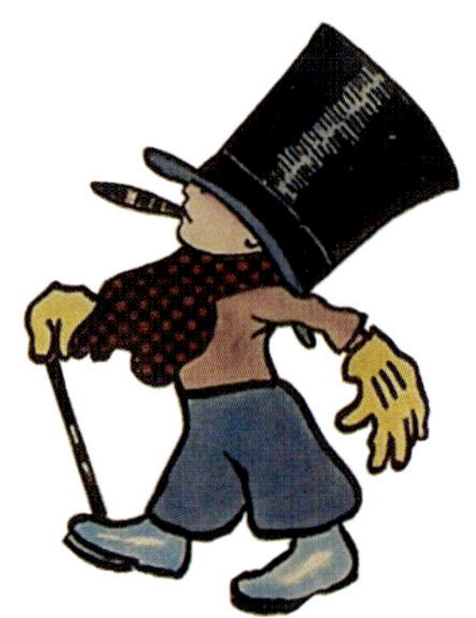

'I see father on Finsbury Park station at about 8:30 a.m., one of the hundreds of business men all wearing the inevitable top hat. It seems funny in these days to think of all those men and all those toppers'.

wrote Phil in 1939

UNLIKE HIS NEPHEW ROBERT, Harry lacked application. An organist's salary was not adequate for his tastes, moreover, and in 1874 he suffered his first bankruptcy. This crisis once resolved, the family moved to Islington where four more children came. No longer a professional musician, Harry was now in the piano business, working as a manager for John Brinsmeads and Sons. *'I see father'*, wrote his son Phil nostalgically in 1939, *'on Finsbury Park station at about 8:30am, one of the hundreds of business men all wearing the inevitable top hat. It seems funny in these days to think of all those men and all those toppers'*. In 1889 Harry patented his own device for 'the improvement in music desks and panel fronts for pianofortes and American organs'. There is no indication that this was a profitable venture, but it is a testimony to his ingenuity and his Mr Micawber-like optimism.

By 1885 finances had markedly improved and the family moved to a large house in New Barnet, where there were connexions, three of his unmarried cousins later establishing the highly successful Lyonsdown School. Harry's house had three extensive gardens on differing levels, in the third of which was a large tree with a platform near its top. At the time of the 1897 Jubilee, it was here, according to Harry's youngest son Norman, that *My father, who was always full of invention, decided to outdo all of his neighbours in the magnificence of his illumination. So he rigged up the old Japanese umbrella [brought back from the Orient by his father-in-law] in the tree about the height of the 'Crow's Nest' and put behind it a large oil lamp and the effect was – to my small mind at least – stupendous. Alas, it was the last function the umbrella performed for, before it had been taken down, a violent thunderstorm broke on it, and when the storm was over the tree was just littered with small bits of coloured paper and a few tragic bamboo ribs stuck out in all directions from the spot where once had been the triumph of illuminations.*

Harry did indeed have an abundance of imagination and ingenuity, as his envelopes would later show, but practicality was not his forte.

...the poor old man in tears behind his bars, and a warder listening to all our talk. But I cannot leave Father in Holloway. The sequel must be recorded that his only possible course was to file a petition in bankruptcy.

wrote Norman In his autobiography

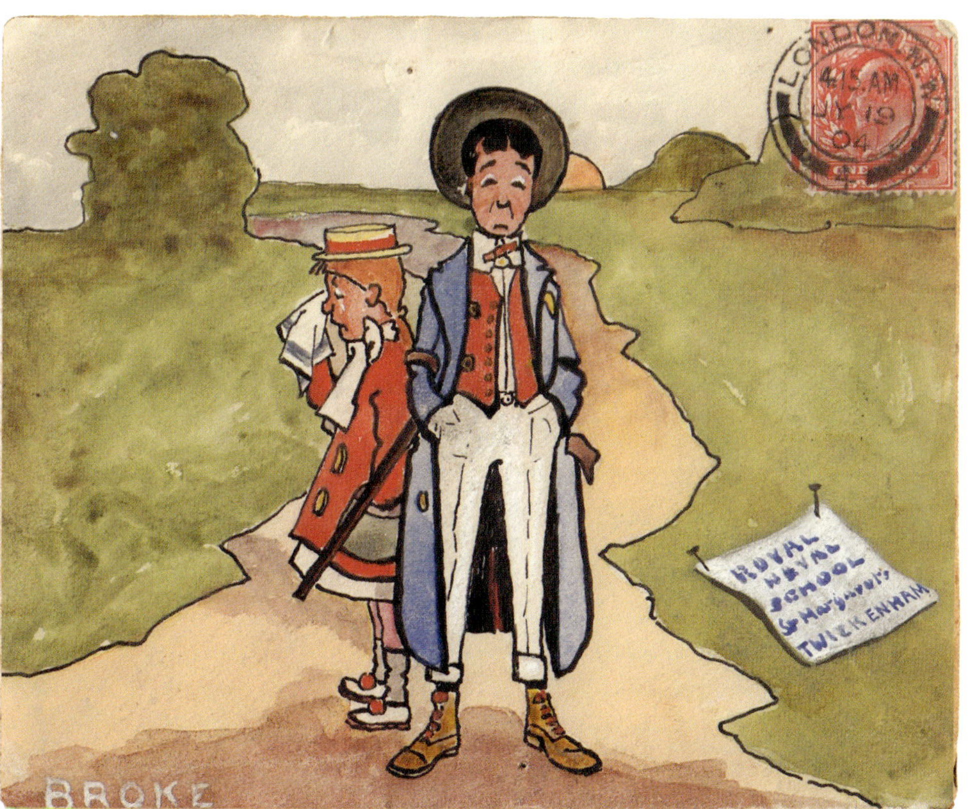

Writing to Jemima in 1859 from Hong Kong her father James Leys observed:

'I am glad to see you are at such a good school and I am sure you will be by and by a very good Scholar'.

She lived up to her father's expectations and in 1883 was appointed Lady Governess of the Royal School for Naval and Marine Officers' Daughters, of whom she was of course one. She was imperious in her manner but was particularly harsh with her nieces when they were boarders at the school. Their father's caricature of her as a dumpy old maid must have particularly appealed to his daughters.

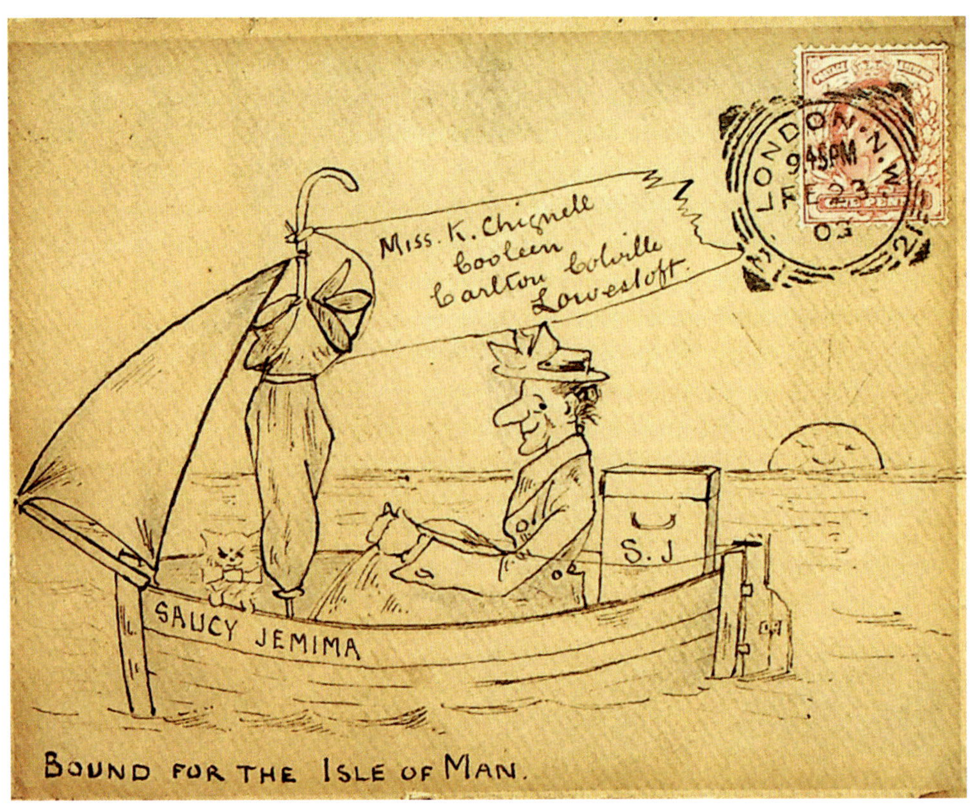

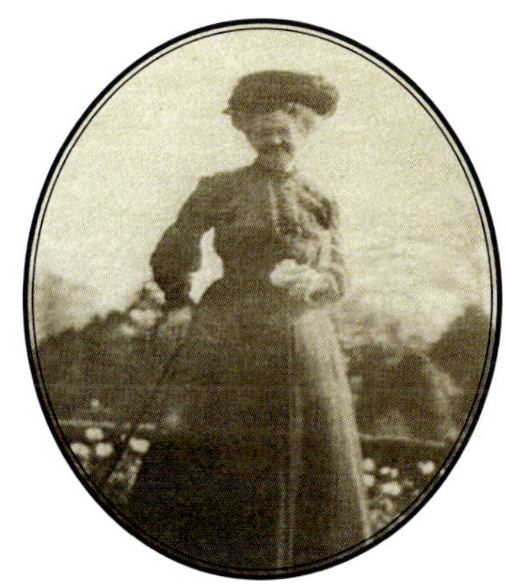

'Miss Leys' father had been a Royal Naval Officer and she ran the school in much the same way as a captain runs his ship'.

From an obituary for Jemima published in *The Royal Naval School Magazine*

DURING THE YEARS following the move, most of the children were away at school: Arthur was at Magdalen College School, Oxford, as was Phil briefly after a number of years at the Choir School of St George's Chapel, Windsor, and three of the girls, Isabel, Kittie, and Ruth, were boarders at the Royal School for Naval and Marine Officers' Daughters in Twickenham where Jemima was Lady Governess. Norman, on the other hand, became a day boy at Merchant Taylor's School in London as a result of his mother's machinations, ('my father having had no plans at all' for his future) and Madge was educated locally.

Soon, however, matters deteriorated again and Harry was reduced, as Norman later put it, '*to peddling pianos and other musical instruments and he rarely appeared on the scene.*' When at home he spent his time in the 'Bungalow' he had constructed for himself in the second garden, as well as indulging his children to extravagent teas in local restaurants. For Phil, who was at Windsor, there were special treats: '*Whatever our father was or was not, he was certainly a generous man and I remember that my Christmas parcel or hamper was always one of the best, [including] a bottle of whisky for the schoolmaster and a bottle of port for the matron*'. Eliza, her own money long since dispersed, had meanwhile established a small school in the house: '*It began in the first place*', wrote Norman, '*by her teaching my sisters Ruth and Kittie but later on it developed until she had some dozen children, mostly boys, as well as an assistant*'. In spite of Eliza's best efforts, however, the financial situation could not be saved and in 1899 the household was broken up. It seems likely that Harry and Eliza, who were temperamentally incompatible, never lived together again, she briefly taking positions as a companion, so it appears, whereas he, according to Norman, '*had no base at all, but travelled about on his business continually*'.

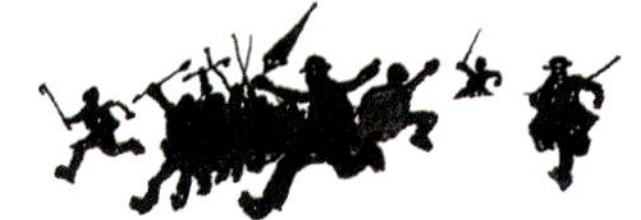

IT WAS THIS LIFE of constant travel that would be the inspiration for the envelopes. They were in many respects a way of keeping the family together as the members went their separate ways, the envelopes tracking their journeys. Arthur moved to Australia where he was ordained. He was soon joined by Isabel who would remain in Australia for the rest of her life in spite of a number of trips back to England, as well as to Canada, and latterly to Rhodesia. In 1897, Phil was made assistant organist at Norwich Cathedral. In the following year he founded the Lowestoft Madrigal Society, soon afterwards becoming organist at St Peter's, Kirkley. It was through his Lowestoft connections that he obtained for his sister Kittie a position as a governess until she left for Canada in 1903 to join her fiancé Charles Henry Chaston, a rancher in the North West Territories. Madge married Herbert Crimp, conductor, composer and organist at Holy Trinity Church in New Barnet who soon afterwards took a position at Leominster Priory Church. Ruth trained at Bishop Otter College in Chichester where, after other positions in different parts of the country, including the Royal School for Naval and Marine Officers' Daughters, she returned as Head Mistress of the primary school.

The disruption was hardest on Norman who, through his mother's efforts, was soon to apply to Clare College, Cambridge. There was no indication that Jemima, who had taken Ruth's further education in hand, made any efforts on his behalf as he entered this new phase in his life and in 1902 he decided in desperation to appeal for £20 from his father, who was visiting Madge in New Barnet. Soon after his own arrival, Harry, who clearly had not taken the Micawber principle to heart, had recklessly ventured into the garden and was pounced upon by a Police Sergeant and Constable. By the time Norman arrived on the scene Harry had been arrested and was in Holloway Prison where Norman remembered vividly going to see him:

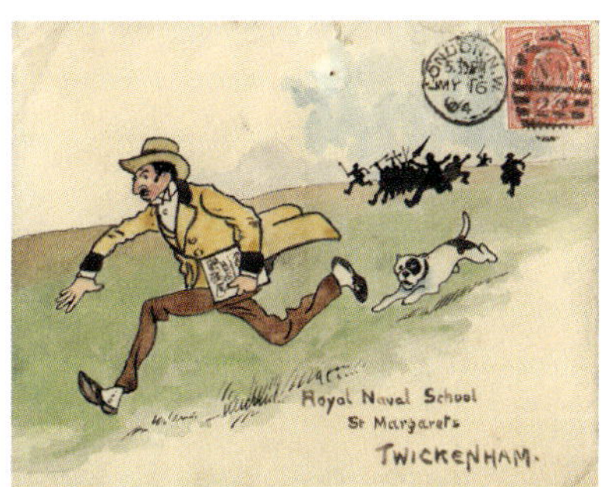

'He was very much broken by it all, but as is so often when things have come to a crisis and the cloud has broken, he soon rallied, and was much relieved by being able to give up his slinking habits in going to and fro'.

...the poor old man in tears behind his bars, and a warder listening to all our talk... But I cannot leave Father in Holloway. The sequel must be recorded that his only possible course was to file a petition in Bankruptcy... He was very much broken by it all, but as is so often when things have come to a crisis and the cloud has broken, he soon rallied, and was much relieved by being able to give up his slinking habits in going to and fro. And in justice to him it must be said that when I finally went to Cambridge, he supported me far better than I ever dared to hope. I think he actually found just about £100 for me during my three years there, and was most generous in some of my extravagances, such as paying my railway fares when I came to London to play Lacrosse, as I did frequently in my last two years.

It is not surprising that Harry would correspond regularly with his children, who themselves kept diaries and wrote regular letters to one another throughout their lives. Apparently they were also assiduous in their correspondence with their parents – to whom they expressed deep devotion in spite of all the vagaries of their childhoods – but few letters survive, the most interesting of which was written to 'my dearest Father' by Arthur on 22 July, 1907, from Port Moresby in Papua where he was to become a missionary:
Today I have seen Papuans for the first time in large numbers. The chief thing that one notices is their wonderful frizzy head of hair. The fashion in clothing is just to have a wisp of coloured stuff as a sort of loin cloth. The women wear only a queer petticoat made of shredded grass, which sticks out all round from the hips. Taking them all through, they are a fine looking race. Harry's response does not survive.

The Tolhurst Collection.

Harry was, nevertheless, not alone in illustrating envelopes. For example Frederick Charles Tolhurst, a Lithographic Artist Journeyman and later Trade Union Secretary from Stockwell, sent more than two hundred comparable envelopes to his children between 1909 and 1940.

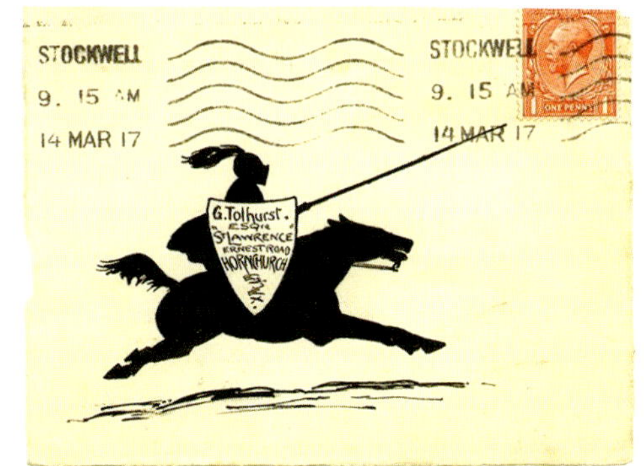

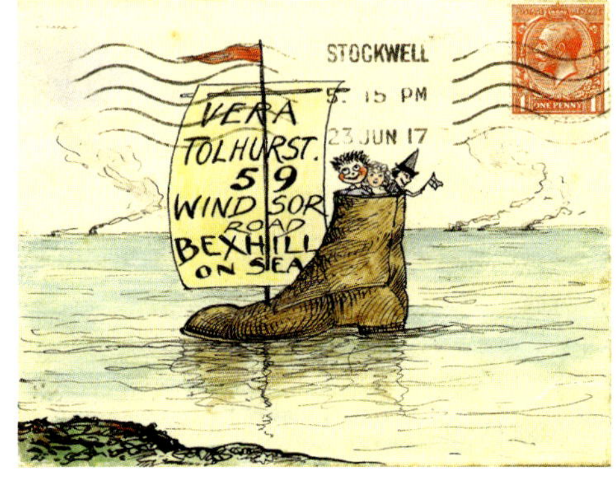

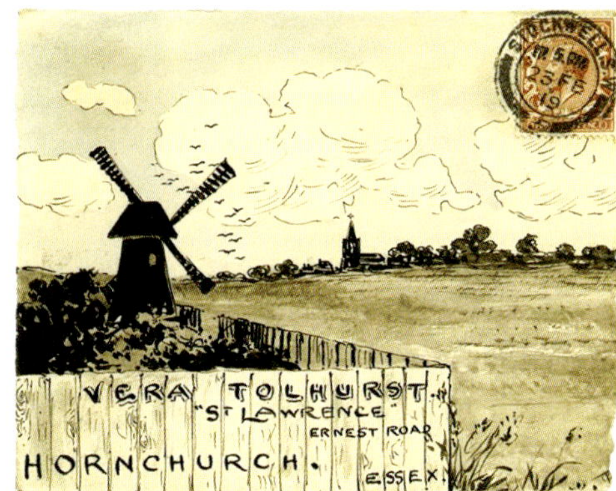

What provoked Harry to turn
workaday envelopes into water-
colour drawings is unknown

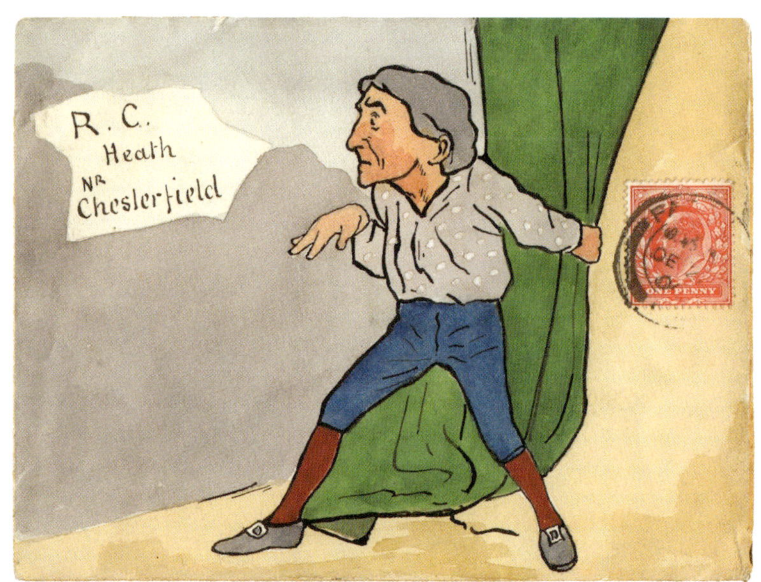

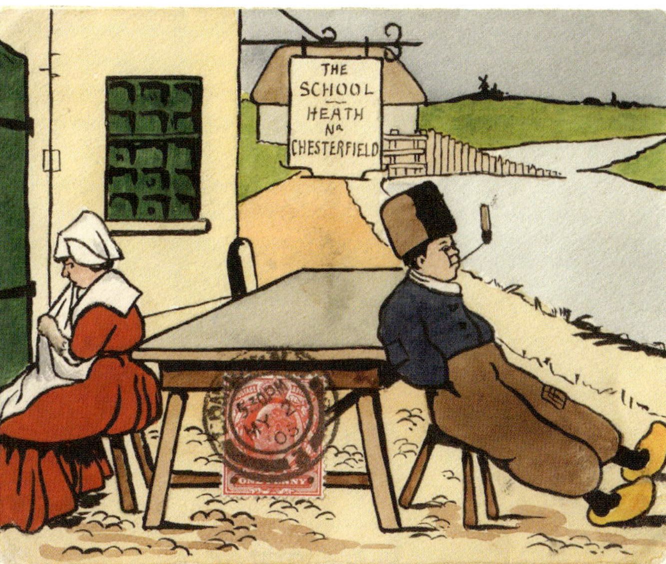

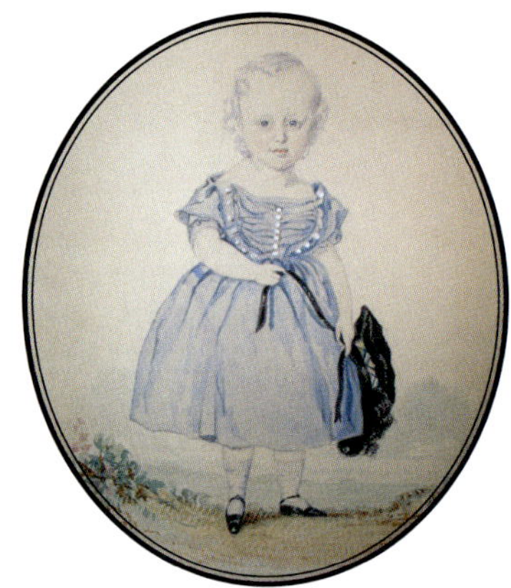

Watercolour of Kittie as a small girl

LETTERS WERE CRUCIAL for this closely-knit but widely-dispersed family. What provoked Harry, however, to turn workaday envelopes into water-colour drawings is unknown. He had in the past painted for his wife and children china with charming scenes, and had produced sensitive watercolour sketches of his children. More to the point, he had presented young Jemima just after his marriage with a book made up of her collection of naval crests which he had linked together in patterns by means of his own drawings. These showed the possibilities of incorporating stamps into a design and in a general sense were the inspiration for the envelopes, much more sophisticated and whimsical, whose first appearance came some thirty years later.

The earliest of Harry's surviving envelopes consists of a pen and ink sketch sent from Glasgow to Madge, by now Mrs Herbert Crimp, on 29 May 1900, just one year after the breakup of the household. It shows a workman in his cap holding a flag in which are embedded two postage stamps. Three years later, to celebrate the birth of Madge's first child, he sent an outsize envelope to his son-in-law in honour of 'A New Barnet Partnership'. Herbert, whose music had recently been featured at the Proms back-to-back with that of Sir Arthur Sullivan, is at the piano wearing tails and playing one of his own compositions, and the baby is on the floor shuffling sheet music, a balloon above him reading: 'That's right father! You make up the toons and I'll stick 'em on paper'.

A number of envelopes were drawn, as this one was, to celebrate births or other significant occasions, but right from the beginning Harry was intrigued by the possibilites of linking scene with address or placement of the stamps. The second to survive, painted on an envelope from MacKay's Commercial Hotel in Glasgow, was sent to Kittie in Lowestoft from New Barnet on 3 August 1902. It shows a smiling young newpaper boy in a cap he

Right from the beginning Harry was intrigued by the possibilites of linking scene with address or placement of the stamps.

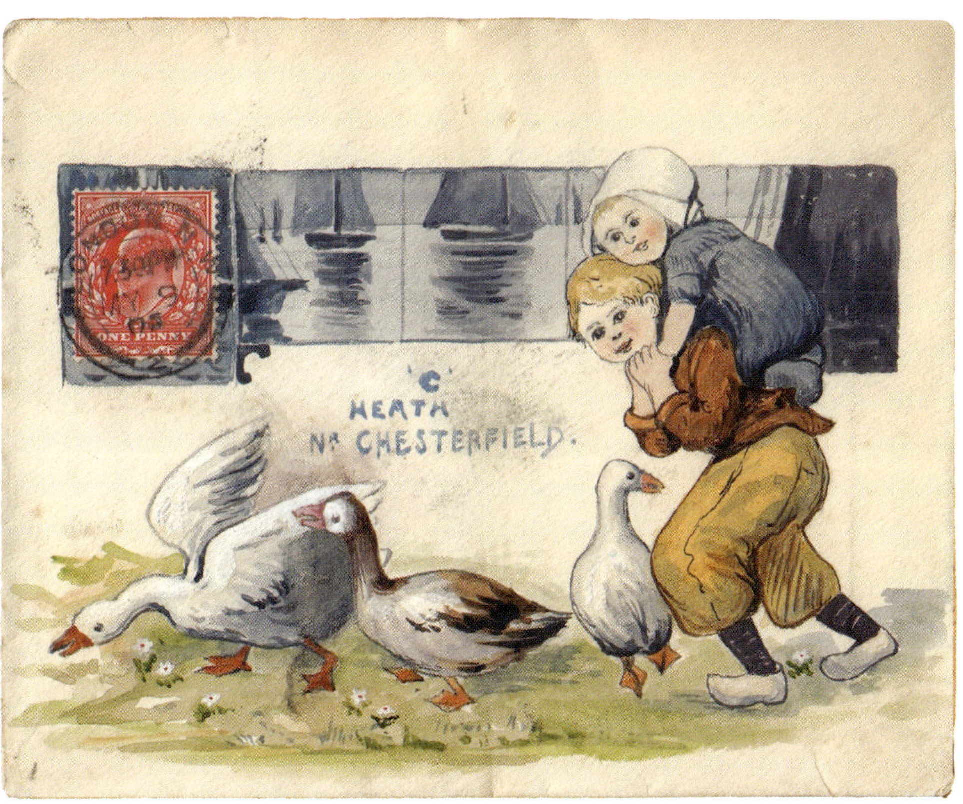

Revised version of second envelope,
sent on 6 December 1902

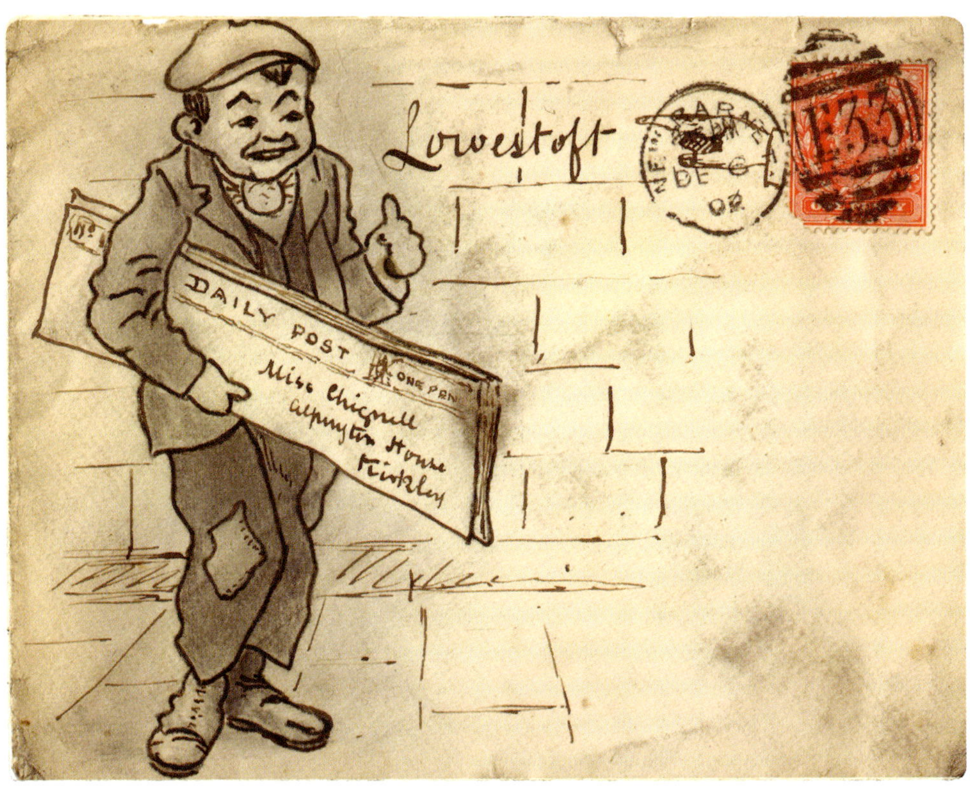

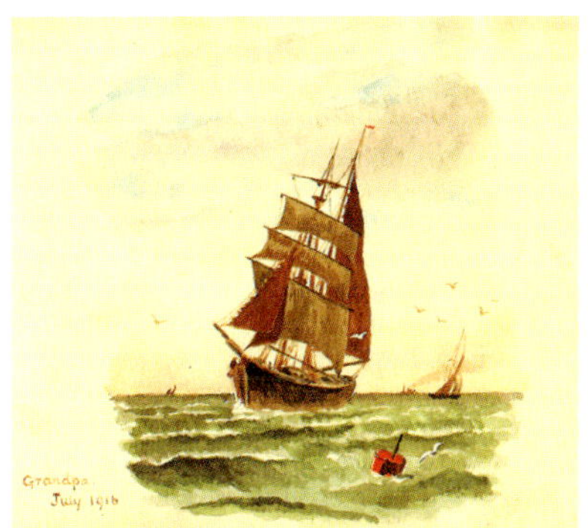

In 1916, while staying with Madge in Leominster, he repeated this design in his eldest grandson's writing album.

is wearing patched trousers and is holding in his left hand a paper which contains Kittie's address. His right thumb points above to the stamp. Over the following months Harry thought more about this design and sent Kittie a revised version on 6 December. Here, the details of wall and pavement are sketched in; the newspaper is shown to be *The Daily Post*; and the boy's thumb points upwards to 'Lowestoft': placing *The Daily Post* on the folded newspaper had made it impossible to include the whole address without crowding.

From this time onwards the designs tended to be duplicated, sometimes appearing in multiple copies. To achieve this, Harry must have kept a pattern book – and he would have learned about this kind of technique from his father's printing business – that he would have carried around with him on his travels, along with a set of water-colour paints. These would have been brought out in the evenings when he was not occupied with his chief passion which was bridge, a game at which all his children excelled as well, Isabel to considerable financial profit. Norman would describe life at the Hampton House Club which was his father's London base as: *'a strange place, rather hugger mugger. Still we could generally get a game of Bridge in the evening and there was an asphalt tennis court where I sometimes played'*.

Harry must have held on to his pattern book after he stopped using the designs for envelopes. An illustration of a sailboat with two masts, a buoy with a seagull perched on it in the foreground, was sent to Ruth in February 1907. Two years later he presented Isabel with a watercolour drawing on a sheet of paper, rather than on an envelope, of the same scene as she prepared to return to Australia after one of her visits to England. In 1916, while staying with Madge in Leominster, he repeated this design in his eldest grandson's writing album.

As we shall see, a number of letters directed to some of the children survive, fewer to others, and none at all to Arthur. We can be sure that all of them would have received very

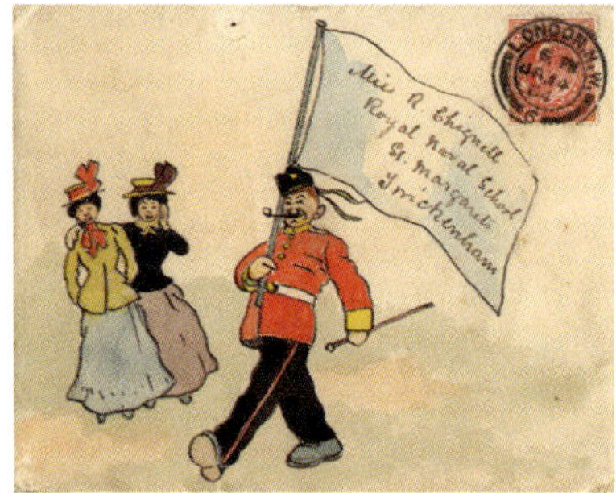

Father could at times write quite good letters but he was generally too busy or too lazy; most of his letters ran to the four sides of a sheet of notepaper and no further.

Phil writing to Isabel in 1929

similar envelopes and in our sections the address does not necessarily correspond to the recipient whose writing we are describing.

None of the letters enclosed in the envelopes survive and no doubt many were duplicates. After all, the family practice was to pass letters from individual to individual as in the case of the one Arthur addressed to 'my dearest father' from Port Moresby on 22 July 1907: it got to Isabel on 26 August, to Harry on 30 September, and on the same day to Eliza, followed by Phil on 2 October, then Norman on 6 October, Ruth on 8 October and finally Madge on 14 October. Some of the envelopes, then, almost certainly contained letters already sent him by one or other of his chidren. In an early example, moreover, he has written on the corner of an envelope sent to Kittie shortly before her departure for Canada: 'A message from Ma(s)' which does indicate as well that he and his wife were still in some sort of communication.

All of Harry's extended family were immensely pleased by the marriage of his cousin Mary Ann to the painter George Vicat Cole about whom one of his cousins would publish a biography in 1896. Vicat Cole's son Rex also became prominent as a landscape artist, as did his son in turn. Given Harry's tendency to experiment with various money generating schemes it seems odd that he did not follow the example of his cousins and turn his artistic talent to profit. This, however, never seems to have occurred to him – perhaps he had become tired of this avocation or perhaps, flighty by temperament, he had moved on to new things – and the last surviving envelope was sent to Phil in Hessle, where he was now church organist, in 1907. The cancellation on the stamp also reads Hessle and this is one of the examples where Harry must have sent an envelope, no doubt with nothing enclosed, from a local post office, stamp and cancellation being the sole reason for posting it. In this case the medium was truly the message!

Although Harry enjoyed incorporating the address and stamp into the design, in witty or ironic ways, sometimes it is the scene itself that stands out. The landscapes, usually of places he had seen himself in his travels or based on photographs and paintings, are beautifully executed. These could easily stand on their own as watercolour drawings. Harry seems to have inherited the talent from his artistic family although he did not develop it.

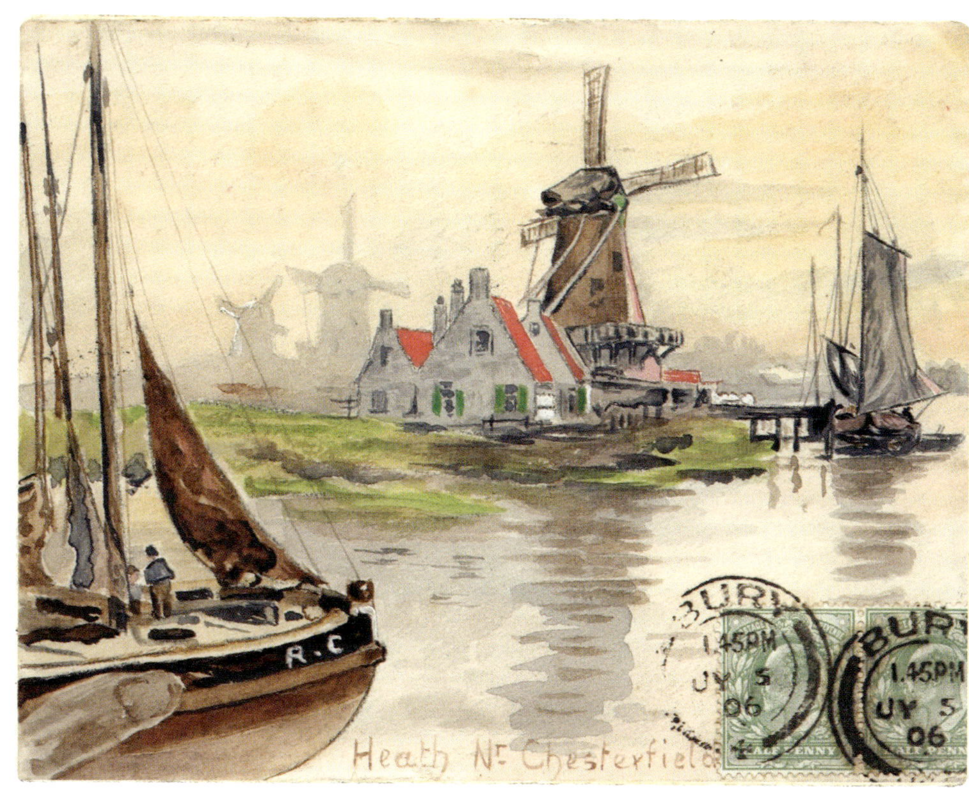

BY THIS TIME Harry's travelling days were coming to an end – he was after all 66 – and he was spending more and more time with his children. Extended stays were not, however, a permanent solution and a thatched cottage was found for him in the village of Shobdon, near Madge in Leominster. Many years later it was described by his nephew Rowland Chignell, by this time a prebendary at Hereford Cathedral, who remembered being taken by his mother to see him in the summer of 1914: '*Uncle's attractive little cottage, thatched and black and white with a garden and lawn, on which he had a cold bath every day, winter included, first thing in the morning*'. Rowland goes on to say that '*he was a dear and very able to talk as naturally to a six year old as to grown ups*'. This same fondness for children manifested itself in a pair of twin envelopes sent to Master Chaston in Canada and Miss M. Jamieson in Australia: they illustrate a group of four children holding their toys, one with thumb in his mouth, marching along accompanied by a goose. The youngest sits behind playing with his rabbit on wheels. Harry's immediate rapport with children was a characteristic he learned during his early visits to Colchester, Mark Rutherford describing their great aunt: '*she was most affectionate to me, and always loaded me with nice things whenever I went to see her. The survival in my memory of her cakes, gingerbread, and kisses has done me more good, moral good – if you have a fancy for this word – than sermons or punishment*'. Rowland, too, would mention treats for tea: '*I do remember that Mother had made him a cake and he was almost cross that she had done so as he had made one for our tea*'.

Like a child himself Harry did not like to be upstaged. Until the end of his life Rowland treasured two of the water colour envelopes from his uncle's collection, 'a great joy to me'.

At the age of 66, Harry's travelling
days were coming to an end.
A thatched cottage was found
for him in the village of Shobdon,
near Madge in Leominster.

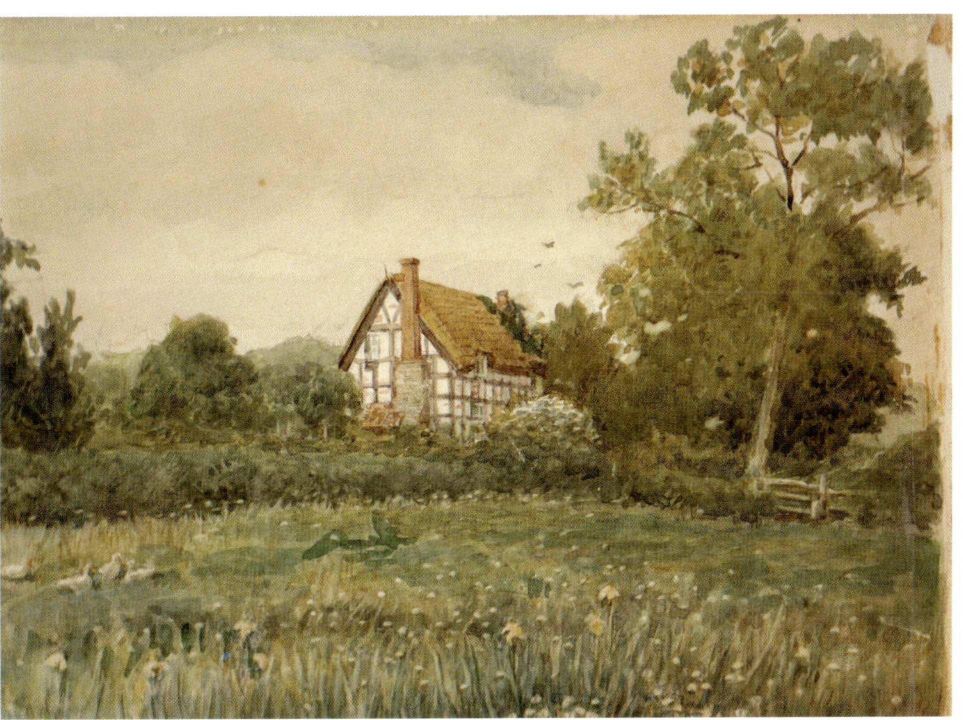

One of a pair of twin envelopes sent to Master Chaston in Canada and Miss M. Jamieson in Australia.

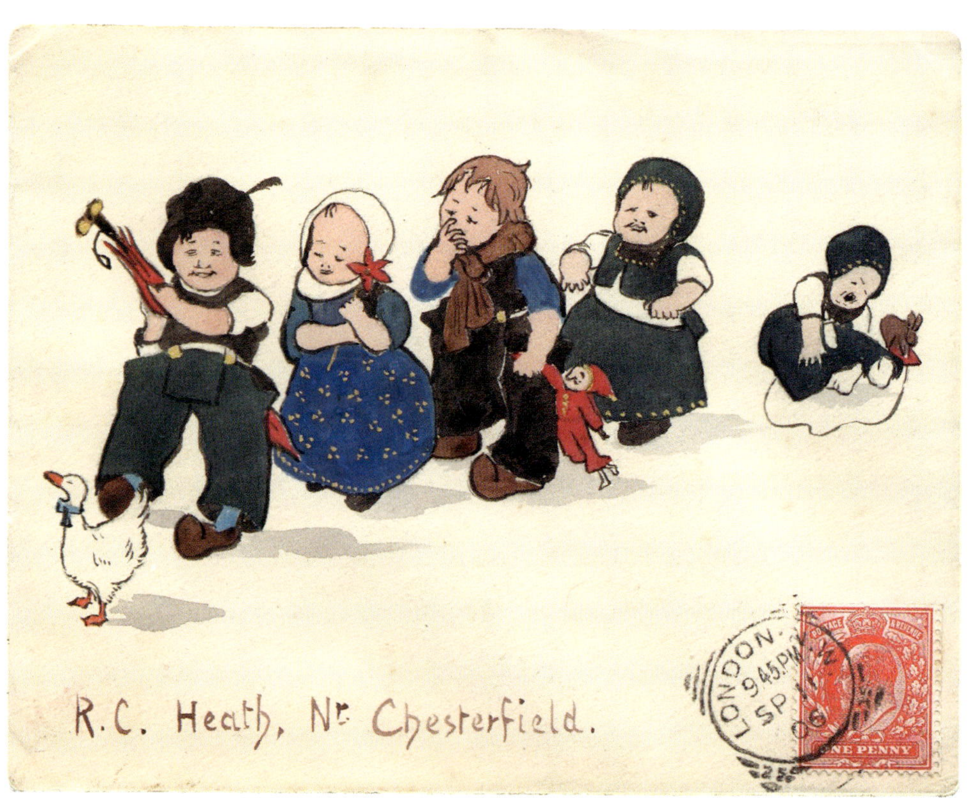

He was a dear and very able to talk as naturally to a six year old as to grown ups.

From a letter by Rowland Chignell, Harry's nephew

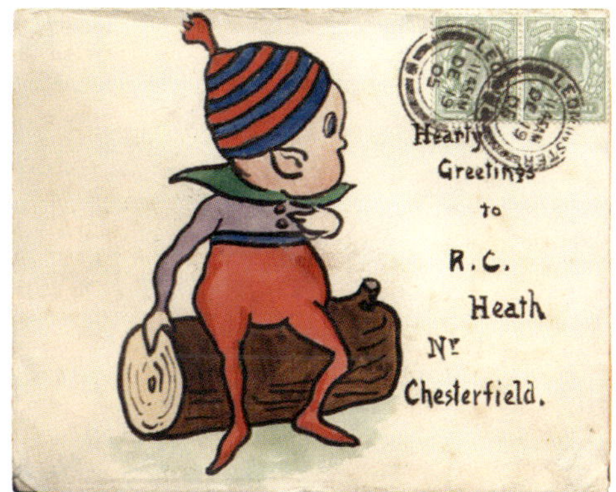

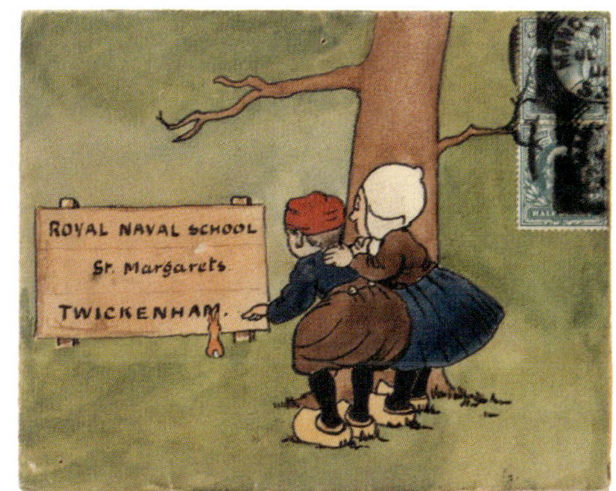

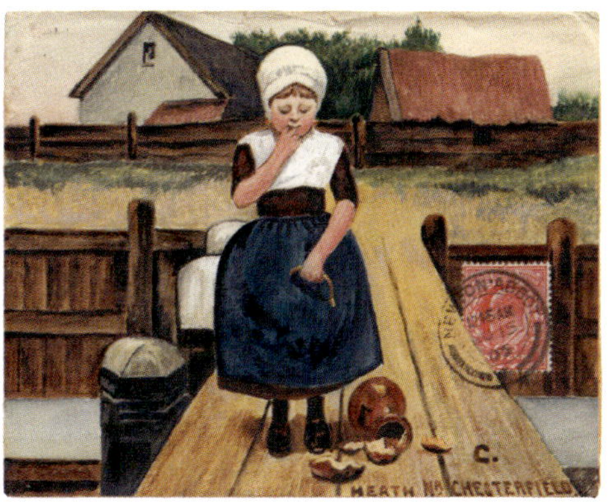

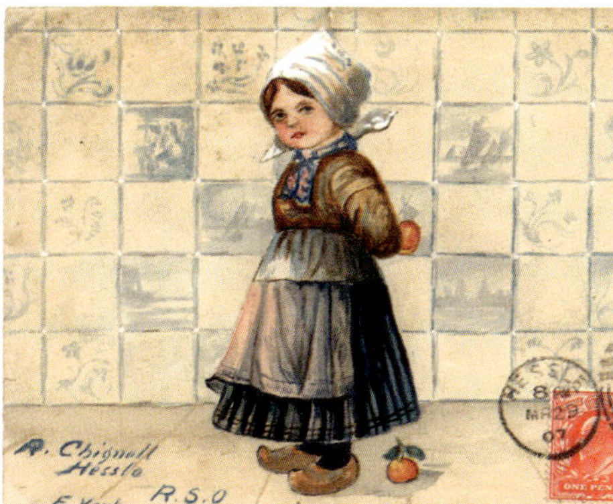

ENVELOPE ART

The life at Shobdon suited Harry well and locals would later recollect him cycling round the village in a carefree manner on his tricycle, sporting a blazer and boater.

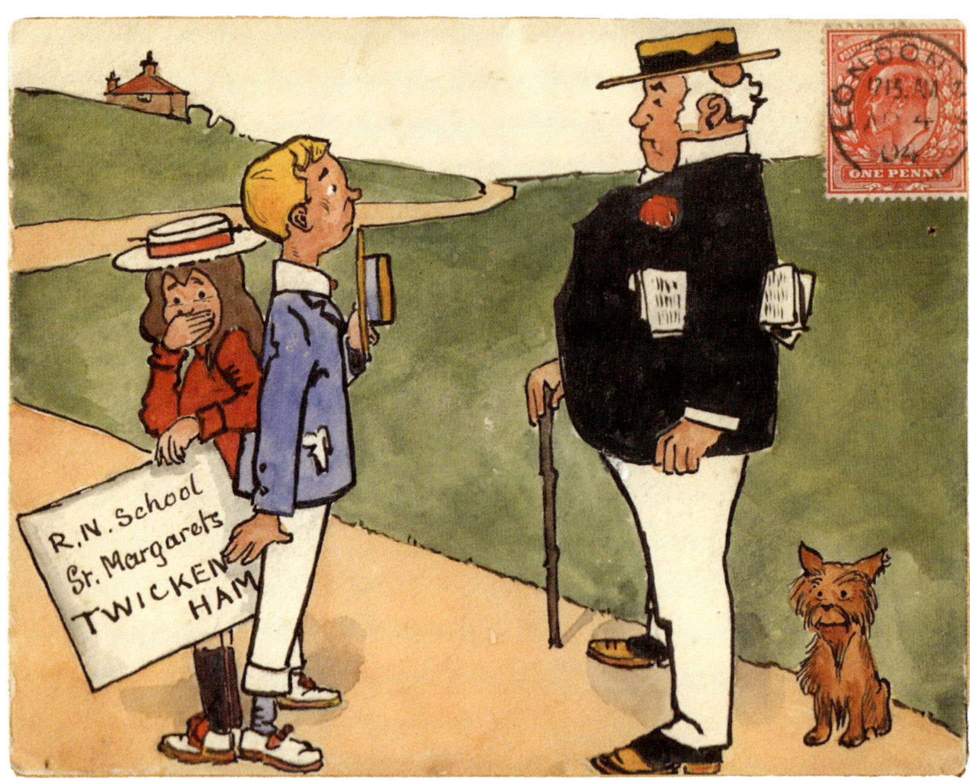

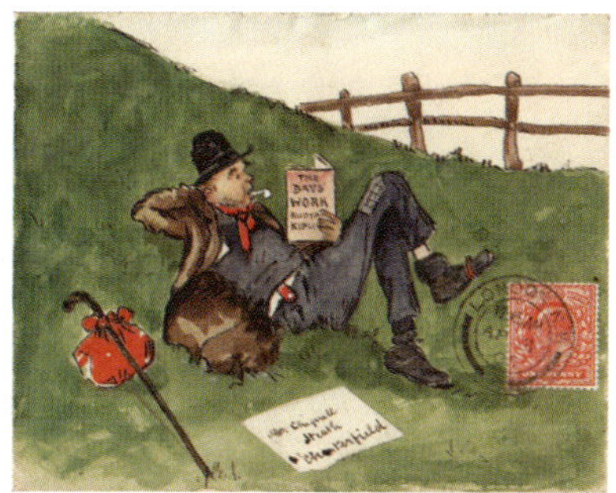

He spent thirteen years at the London Charterhouse with just no cares in the world

THE LIFE AT SHOBDON suited Harry well and locals would much later recollect him cycling round the village in a carefree manner on his tricycle, sporting a blazer and boater. He did continue to sketch from time-to-time during these years and there is, for example, a charming scene in Madge's guest book. Another beautiful watercolour drawing, meticulous in detail, shows an ocean liner on a smooth sea. Given that most of his children spent considerable time on ocean crossings it may well have been painted to commemorate one of their trips.

In 1919 Arthur, who had served as an army chaplain during the war, was appointed Master of the Hull Charterhouse. Norman, meanwhile, was a master and later housemaster of the Saunderites at Charterhouse School. Realizing that their father, who was approaching eighty, was unlikely himself to make plans for the future they secured a place for him among the 'decayed gentlemen' at the London Charterhouse. He was admitted in 1920 and settled in immediately: in Madge's Guest Book there are ironic drawings of himself as a Carthusian monk or in his gown trundling off to dinner. A grandson remembered one of Harry's visits to the Charterhouse School during these years: *'An old man, well into his eighties, with a merry twinkle in his eye and a keen sense of humour, but with a definite tendency towards irascibility'*.

After Harry's death Norman would opine that: *'Father's end was entirely happy. He spent thirteen years at the Charterhouse with just no cares in the world, without really having to think where his next meal was coming from, or being bothered about getting people to make his bed or wash up for him'*.

ALTHOUGH THE SCION of a deeply religious family, as well as having a cousin who was a famous preacher and a son who was a clergyman, Harry, as Norman observed, *'did not conform to the ordinary religious life of most men and seldom went to church. But if not religious he was something of a philosopher in a very practical way, and he had a full measure of the Christian chracteristic of love, though he failed, like most of us, in extending that principle to the people and institutions that he did not like'*. Towards the end of his long life Harry speculated about the afterlife, wondering indeed if there were a future at all. His conclusion was that he could hardly believe in such a thing.

Here, perhaps, we have the essence of the man who had painted his envelopes all those years ago: living in the present, unconcerned about provision for what was to come; ironic; sometimes short-tempered as in the case with his wife and sister-in-law; witty and kind; sentimental – he was regularly reduced to tears – and with a strong eye for beauty, but little perseverance. He was, in other words, a born artist.

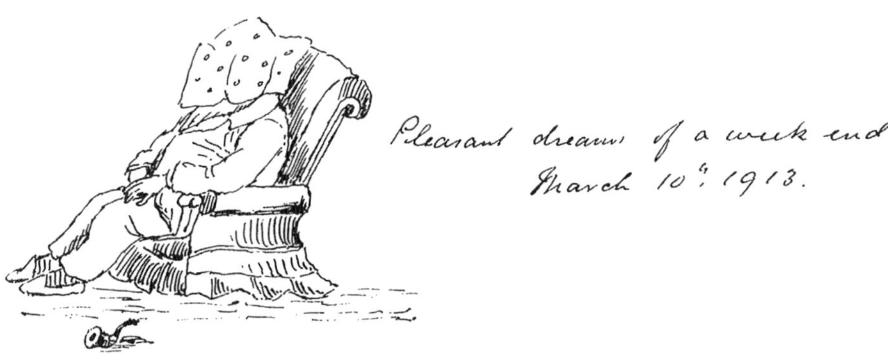

Here, perhaps, we have the essence of the man who had painted his envelopes all those years ago: living in the present, unconcerned about provision for what was to come

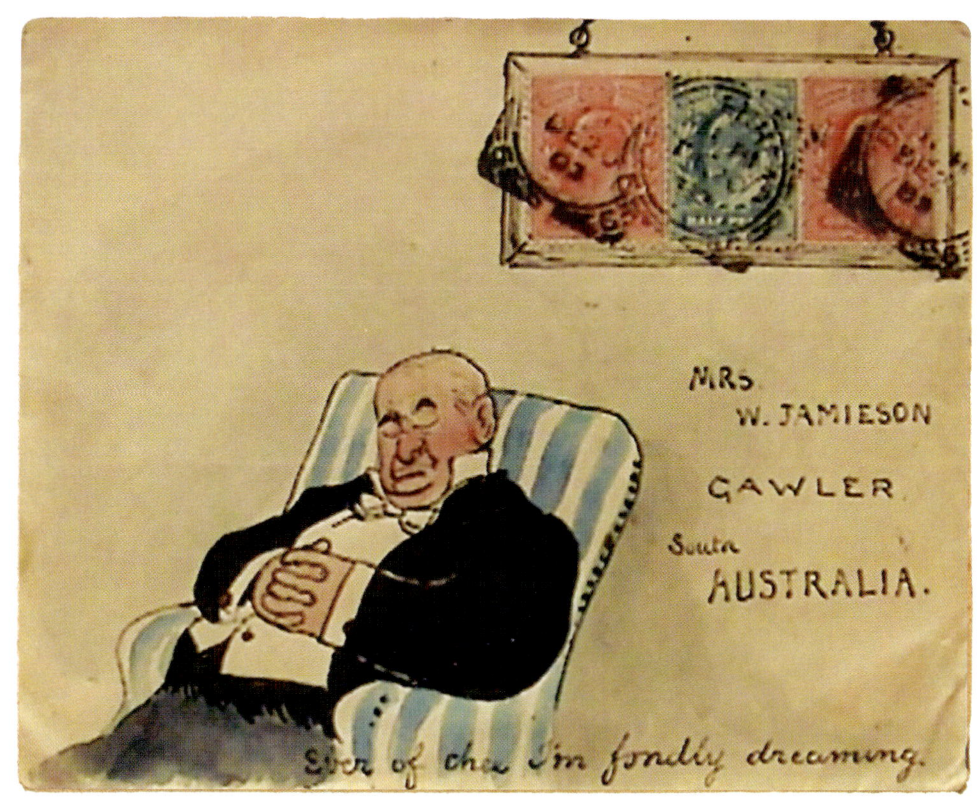

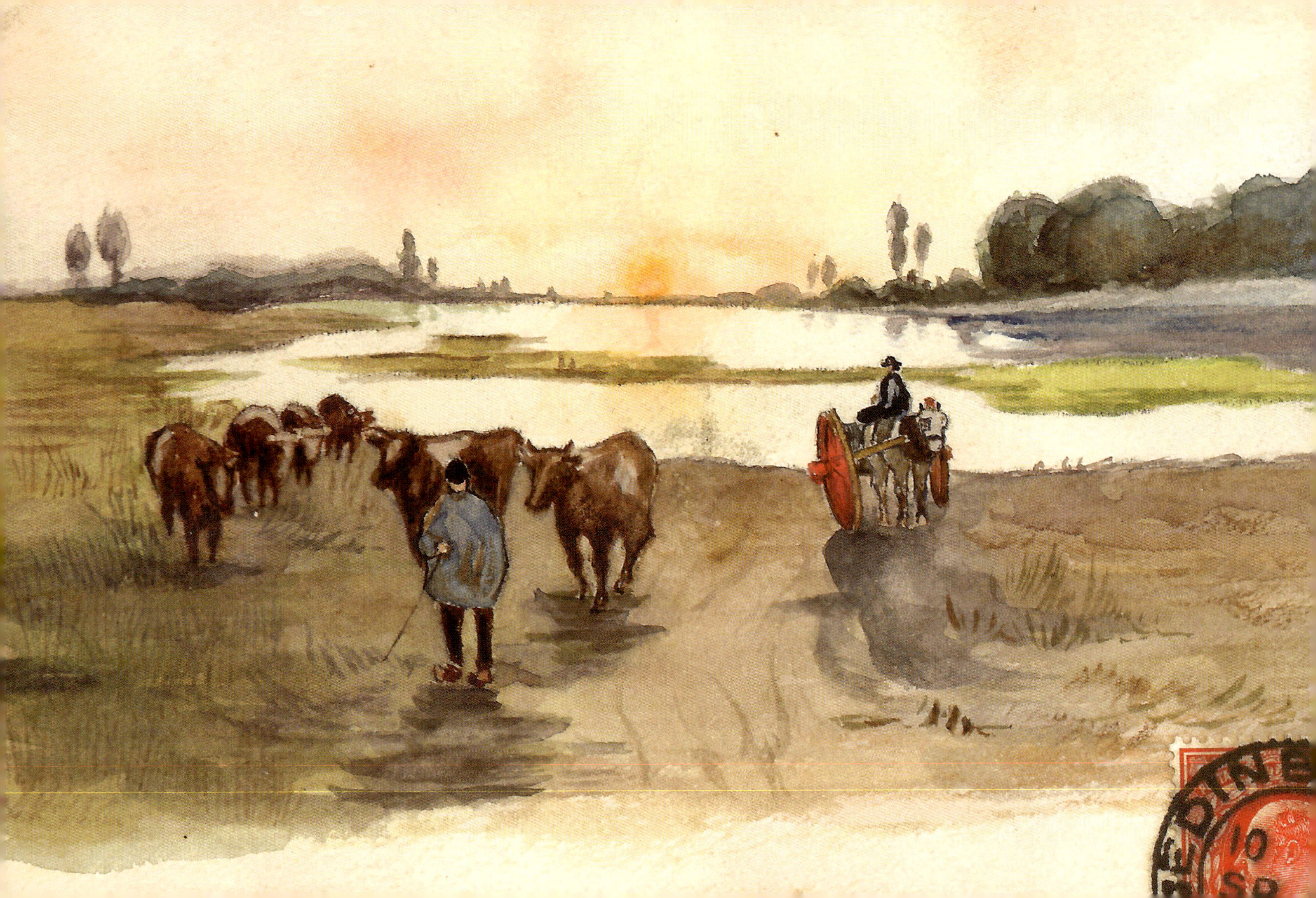

The Recipients

Henry 1841-1933
Centre back row

Arthur 1870-1950
Standing back row left

Phil 1872-1947
Seated back row right

Isabel 1876-1958
Seated middle row left

Norman 1883-1961
On his mother's knee

Eliza 1844-1914
Middle row middle

Madge 1874-1960
Seated middle row right

Kittie 1880-1953
Seated front row left

Ruth 1878-1966
Seated front row right

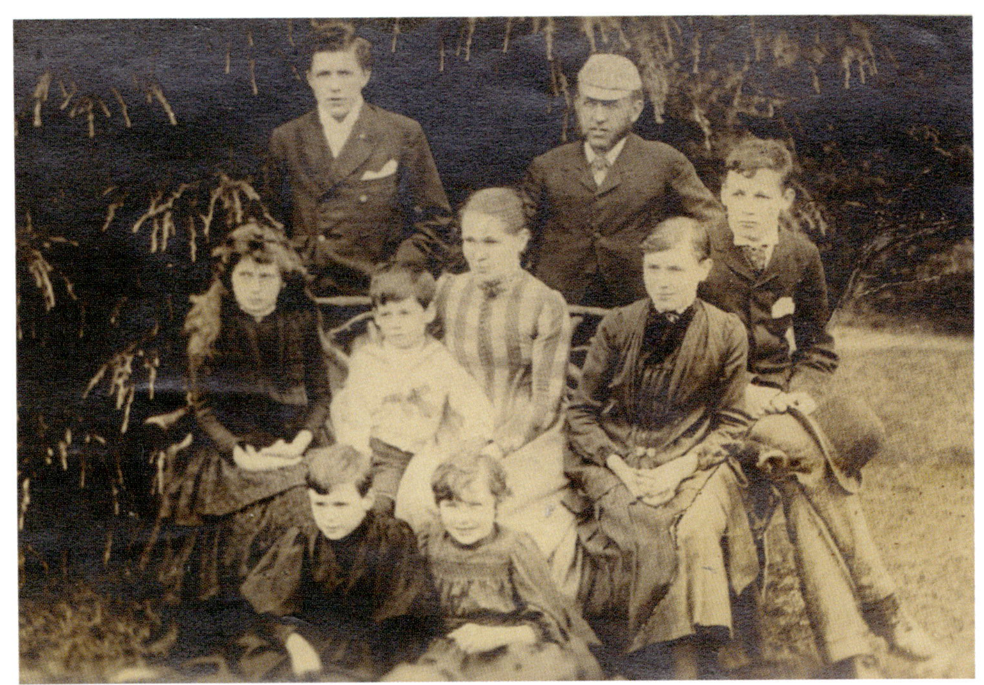

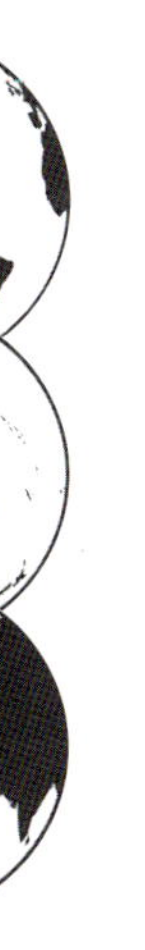

ALMOST THREE-HUNDRED-AND-FORTY ENVELOPES are still intact but an even greater number have been lost or destroyed. For example, none survive from those that must have been sent to **Arthur** in Gawler, South Australia, and then Papua. There is just one to **Phil** in Hessle, but none to him in Norwich or in Lowestoft. To **Ruth**, on the other hand, there are one hundred and fifty; to **Kittie** one hundred; **Norman** fifty-three; and **Isabel** twenty eight. The few sent to **Madge** were addressed to New Barnet; Norman's to New Barnet, followed by Clare College, Cambridge, Hessle, Leominster, and finally Jersey; Isabel's to Gawler; Kittie's Lowestoft, Norwich, and finally Skull Creek, Canada; and Ruth's followed her from school to school as she moved up the teaching ranks. Several were addressed to Eliza.

For the children living abroad, sometimes in primitive conditions, the images of the peaceful world they had left behind must have brought consolation and nostalgia. For Arthur they were also reminders of why he was tempted to question the so-called superiority of the white man's civilization.

In the pages that follow the quoted passages come from Arthur's *An Outpost in Papua* (London, 1911); from Phil's unpublished diary of his travels around the world with the Sheffield Choral Society in 1911 (Phil 1911); and Norman's memoirs of his early years written in the 1930s (cited as *Memoirs*). The reproductions of the envelopes themselves come from the collections of Harry's great grandchildren: Guy Abel, James Carley, Richard Crimp, and Mary Haynes.

Phil,
World Tour

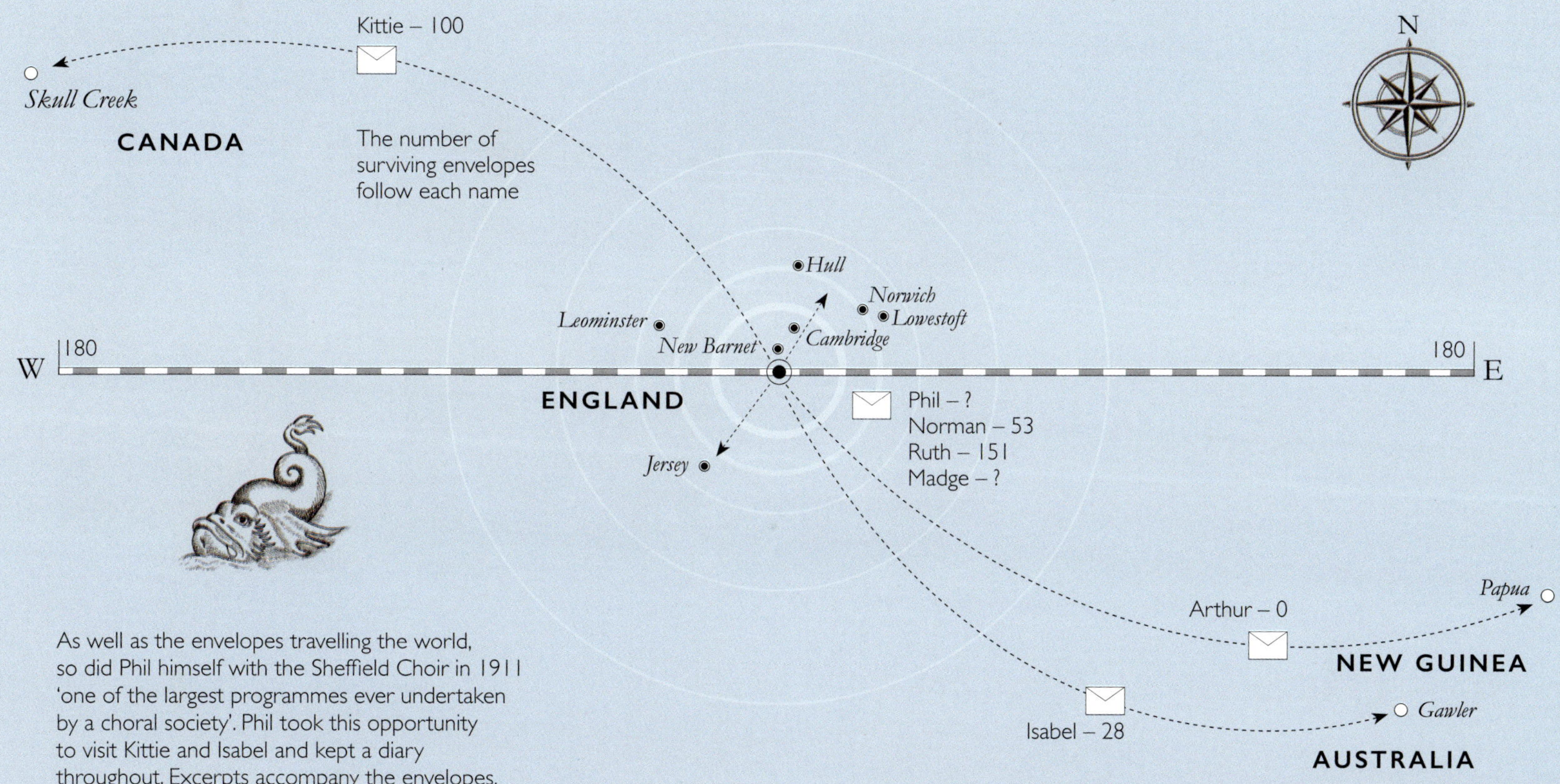
Kittie – 100
Skull Creek
CANADA
The number of surviving envelopes follow each name
N
Hull
Norwich
Lowestoft
Leominster
New Barnet
Cambridge
W 180
180 E
ENGLAND
Phil – ?
Norman – 53
Ruth – 151
Madge – ?
Jersey
Papua
Arthur – 0
NEW GUINEA
Isabel – 28
Gawler
AUSTRALIA
As well as the envelopes travelling the world, so did Phil himself with the Sheffield Choir in 1911 'one of the largest programmes ever undertaken by a choral society'. Phil took this opportunity to visit Kittie and Isabel and kept a diary throughout. Excerpts accompany the envelopes.

WORLD TOUR

Phil, *Sheffield Choir*

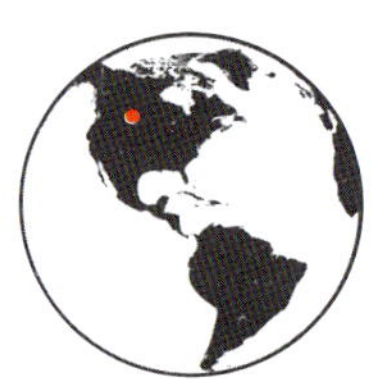

Starting from Liverpool on March 17 [1911] Dr Henry Coward's Sheffield Choir of 200 singers will make a tour of the world – one of the largest programmes ever undertaken by a choral society. The choir will make an extensive tour of Canada and the United States, afterwards visiting Australia, New Zealand, and South Africa.

Adelaide Advertiser, 1911

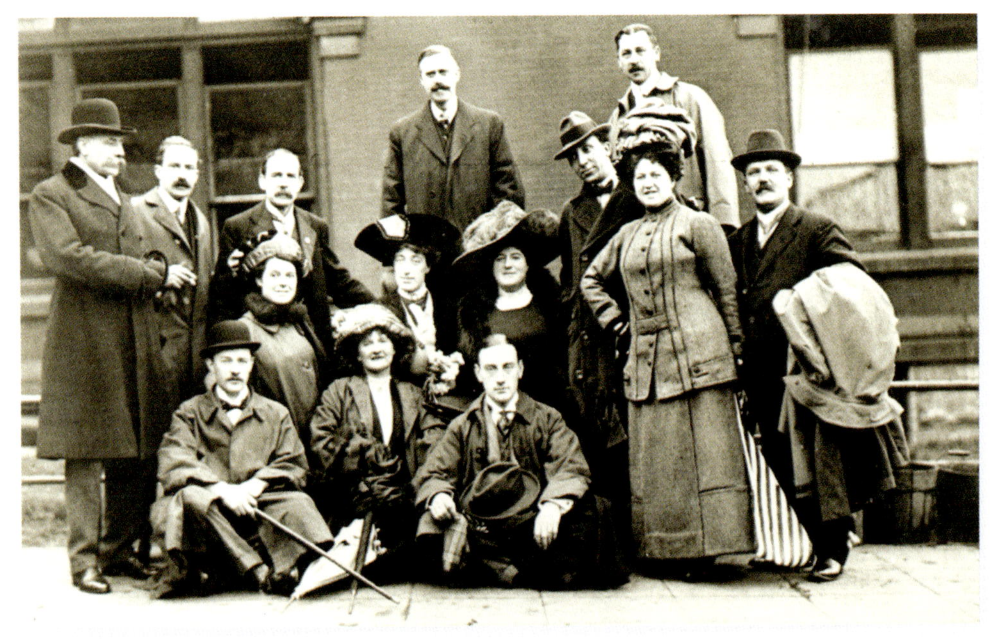

Sir Edward Elgar, back centre, will accompany the choir to Canada and the United States with Dr Henry Coward and Dr Charles Harriss will act as conductor.

At last we are on shore. –
AMERICA – and what awful roads.
– nothing but hard frozen snow,
wooden planks for a path, and
wooden houses of all shapes and
sizes for streets, the telephone poles
at all angles, not one being by any
chance actually upright: – the roads all
crooked and irregular, and the shops
very big and empty looking.

Phil arriving in Halifax
24 March 1911

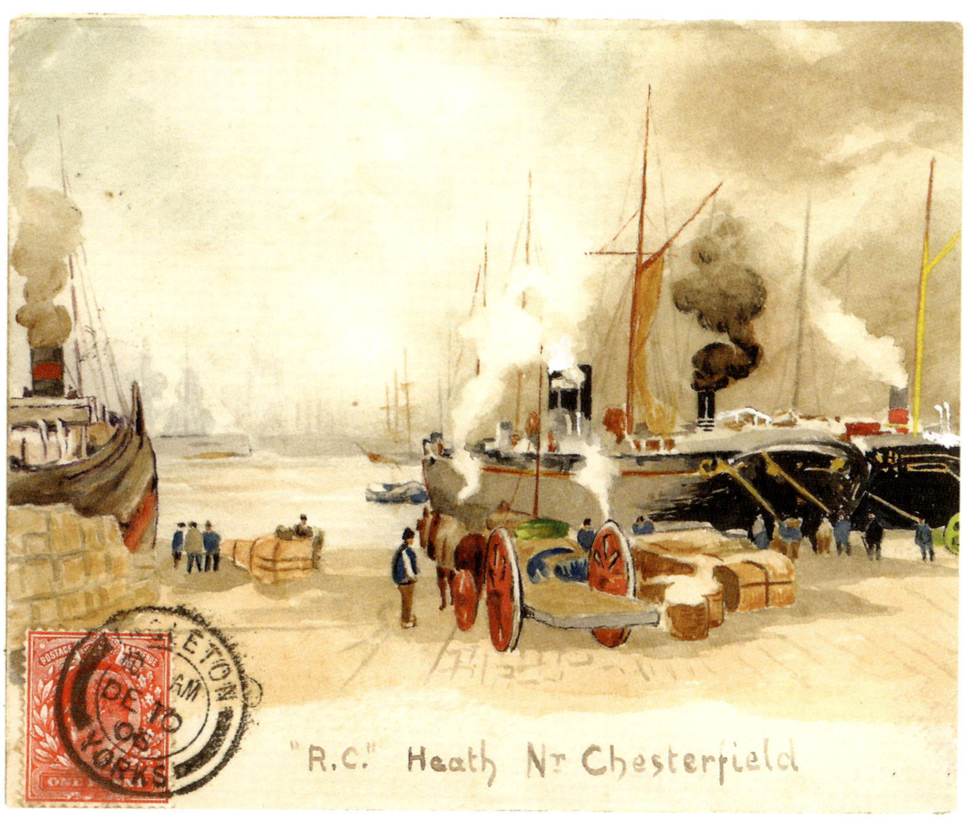

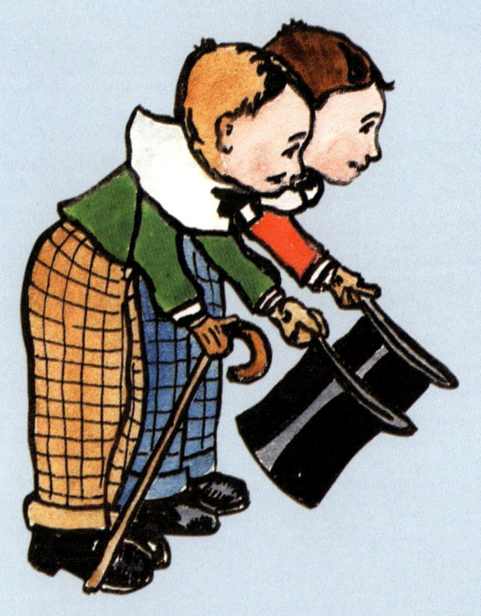

A hasty breakfast, then off to the Massey Hall for a rehearsal of the 'Dream of Gerontius'. We find Sir Edward Elgar with the Baton, and he gets a hearty greeting from us. The rehearsal is a very formal affair, the work being taken straight through, with only periodical comments or instructions.

The Sheffield Choir Toronto (April 4)

A mail bag awaits us in the hall, — a huge one, by the way, for we have been without letters since we left the old country. It takes two of our stewards two hours to sort the letters, which we find ready for us in alphabetical order in the large cloak room. There is an interesting quarter of an hour, when everyone is opening and reading letters, and then a general movement is made back to the hotel for lunch.

The Sheffield Choir
Toronto (April 4)

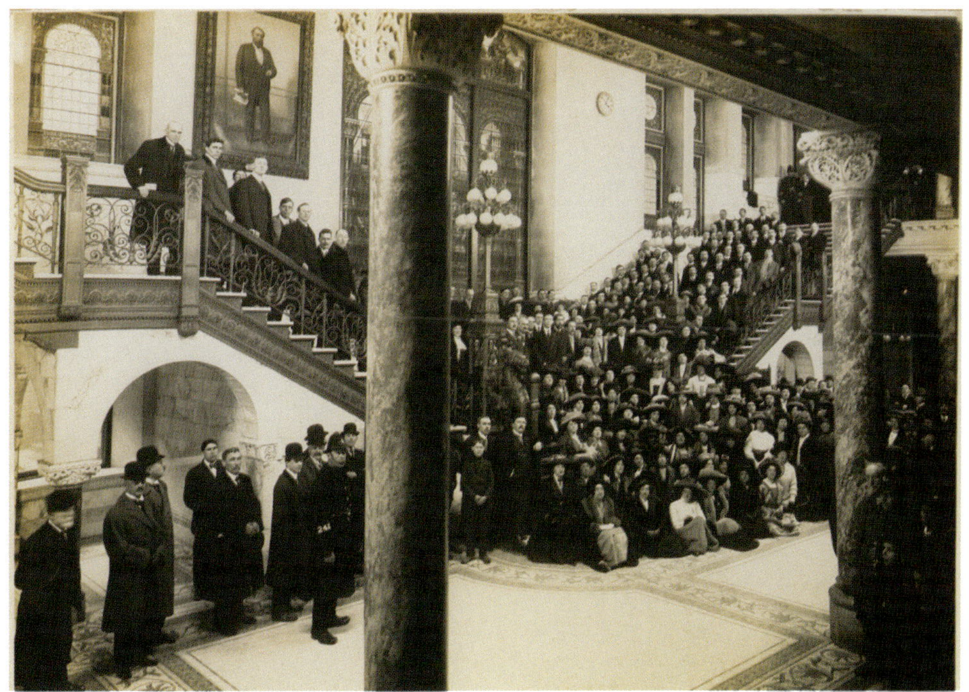

Kittie,
Skull Creek, Canada

CANADA

Kittie, Skull Creek

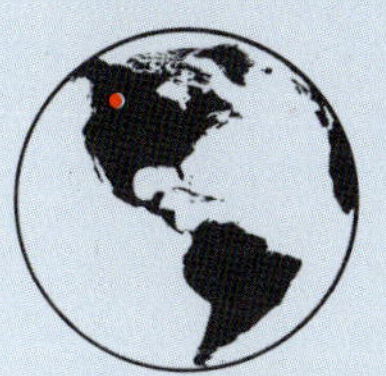

The early letters to Kittie are addressed to the Assa, North West Territory.

On 1 September 1905 the province of Saskatchewan was created and henceforth the new address was used.

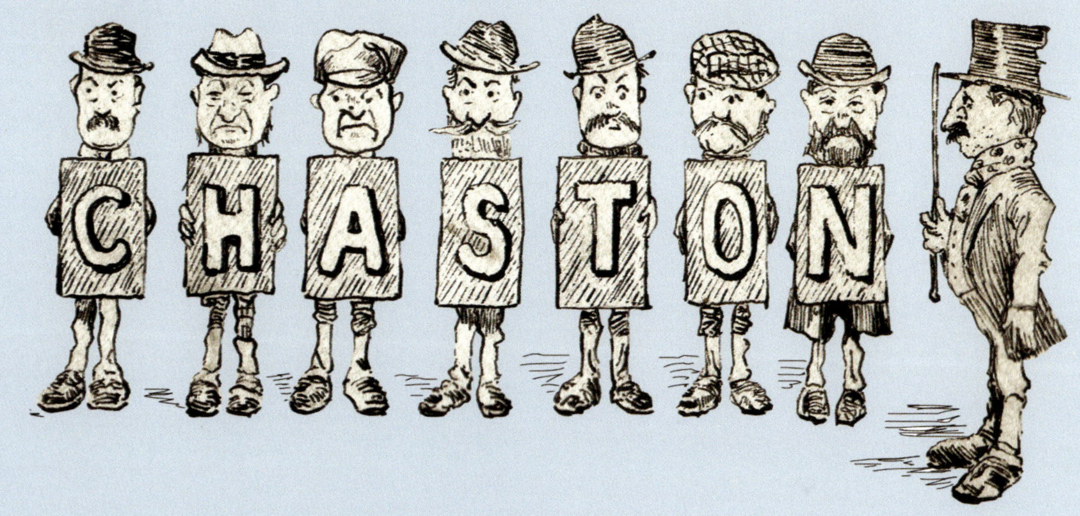

I am expecting a visitor in Moose Jaw; Kittie's husband Charles Chaston whom I have not previously met. He has travelled 130 miles or so to meet me, and to hear our choir sing. We are soon on brotherly terms. Coming out of the hall we find a dust storm raging, and most of us get dust in our eyes and ears and noses and mouths, and even on the train we find very little relief.... A little later we are on the great Trans-continental train, which takes people from East to West America in about a week... Charlie and I leave the train at Gull Lake exactly at the time due, 7.45 am.

Moose Jaw – May 6

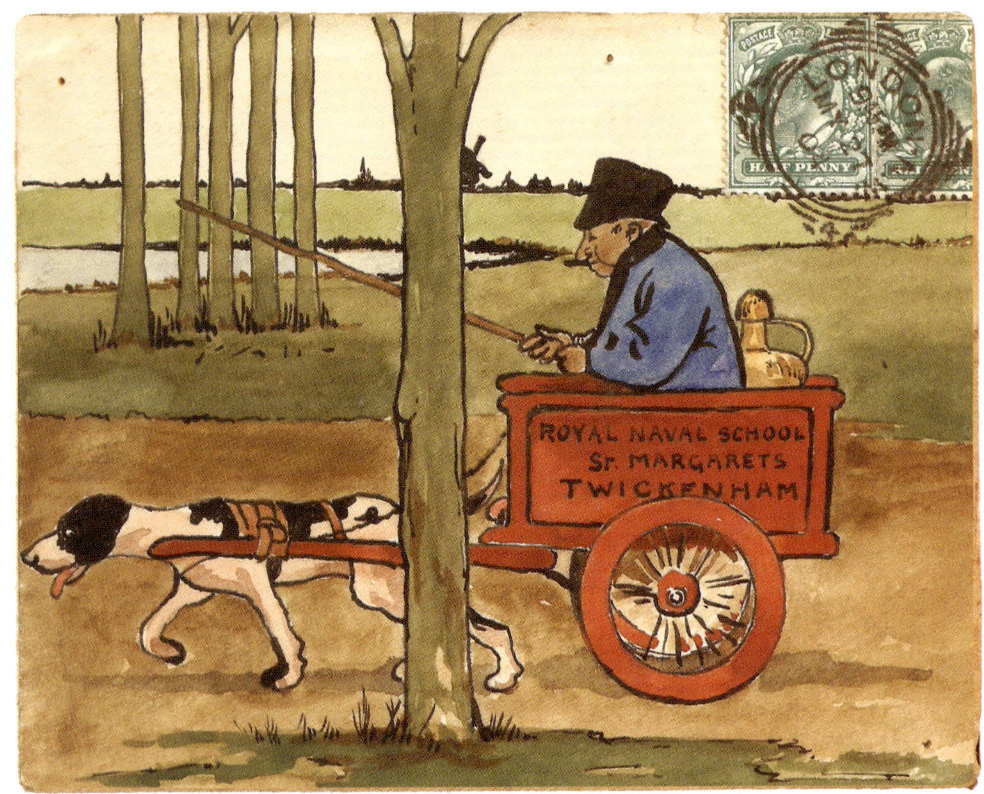

Five minutes walk up the hill and along a broad pathway or sidewalk brings us to the house, where Kittie meets us, and her three younger children. Kittie has changed but little since I last saw her, eight years ago, perhaps a little bit more the woman that is all...

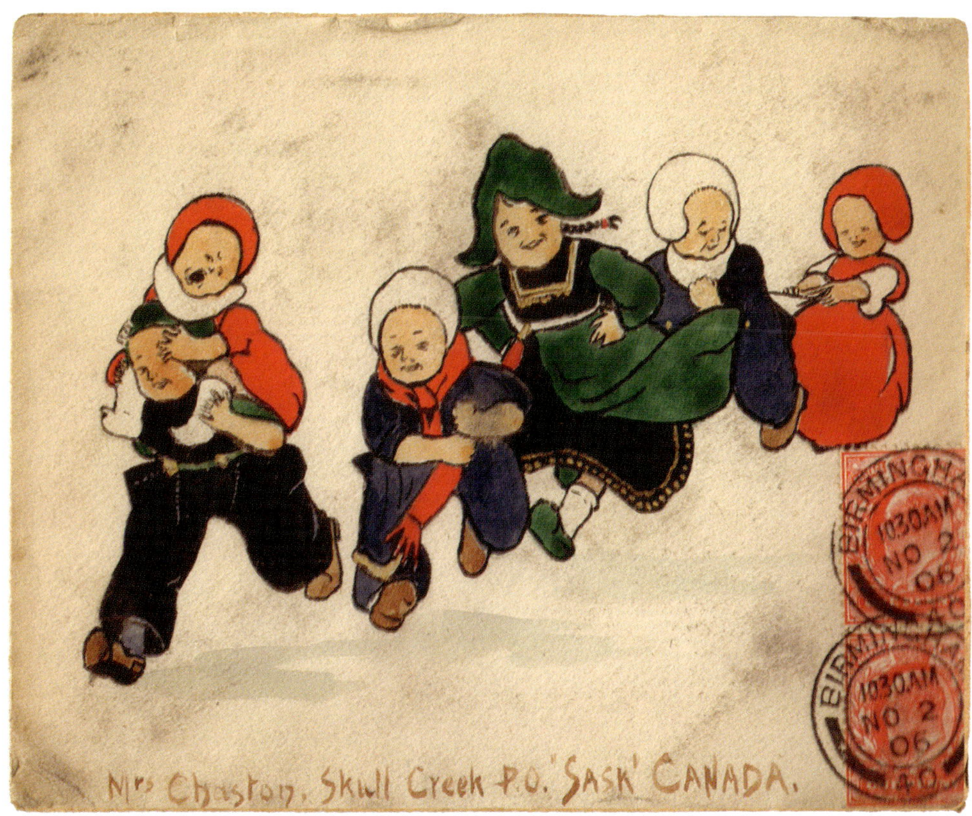

...The house is built of old telegraph poles laid sideways and plastered up together, and sawn off to make room for doors and windows. Really this idea of construction is pretty and a delightful contrast to the plain wooden cottages and sheds all around. I can hardly realize that I am now so far from England and home, for this little house in Saskatchewan is just as English as anything one could find in the Old Country'.

Phil arriving at Gull Lake Saskatchewan to see Kittie

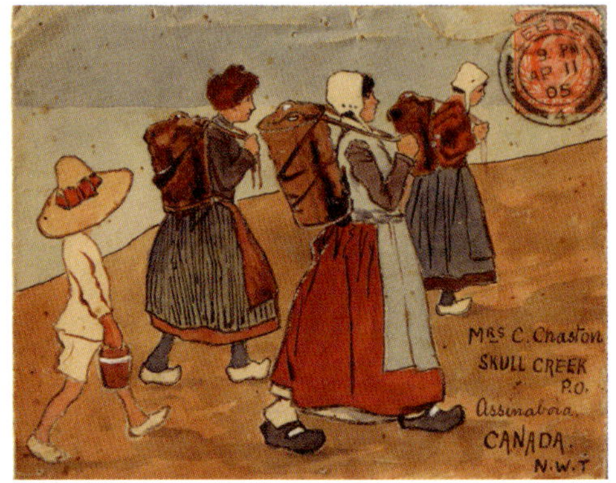

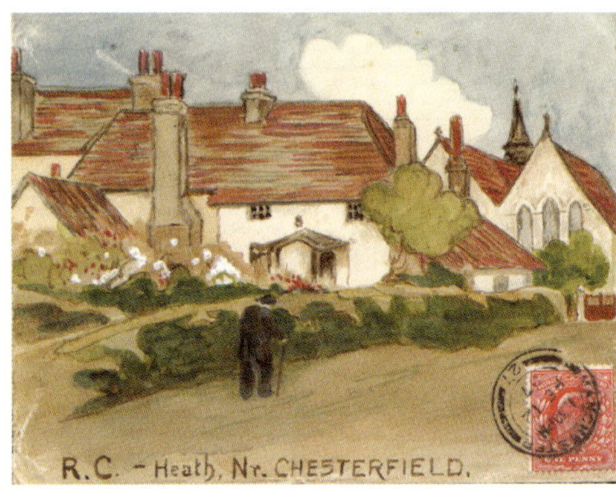

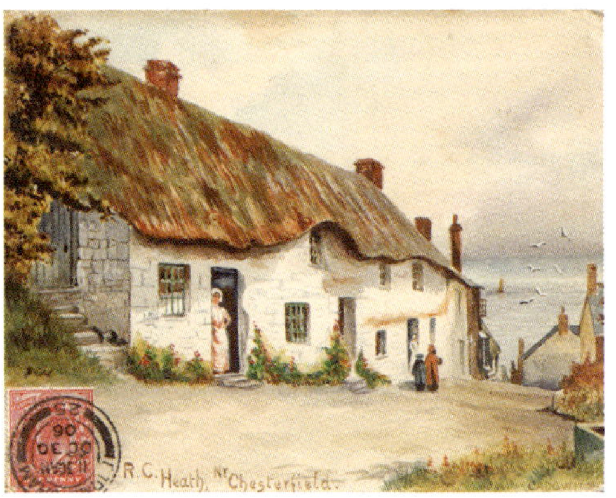

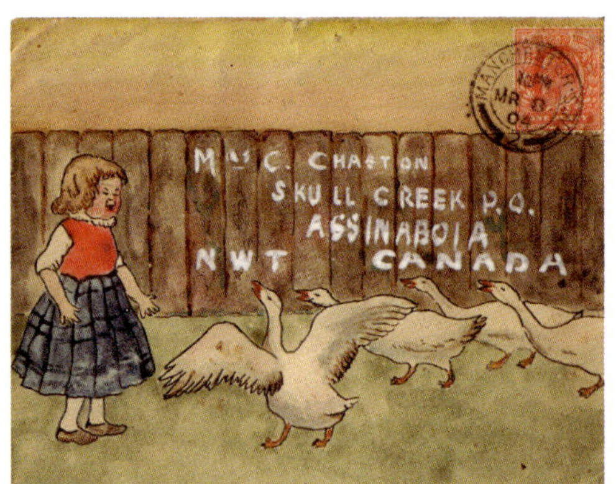

My brother-in-law takes me for a long ride out into the country, where he has some business and we drive about 12 miles due south.

At the top of a hill the trail strikes across open land, which now and then is ploughed up, the plough having crossed field and road alike, so that sometimes one has to guess the direction of the accepted road or trail. We see a steam plough patchwork on an expanse of virgin land, lands that have never, to this day, borne grain or fruit, or been of the least service to mankind.

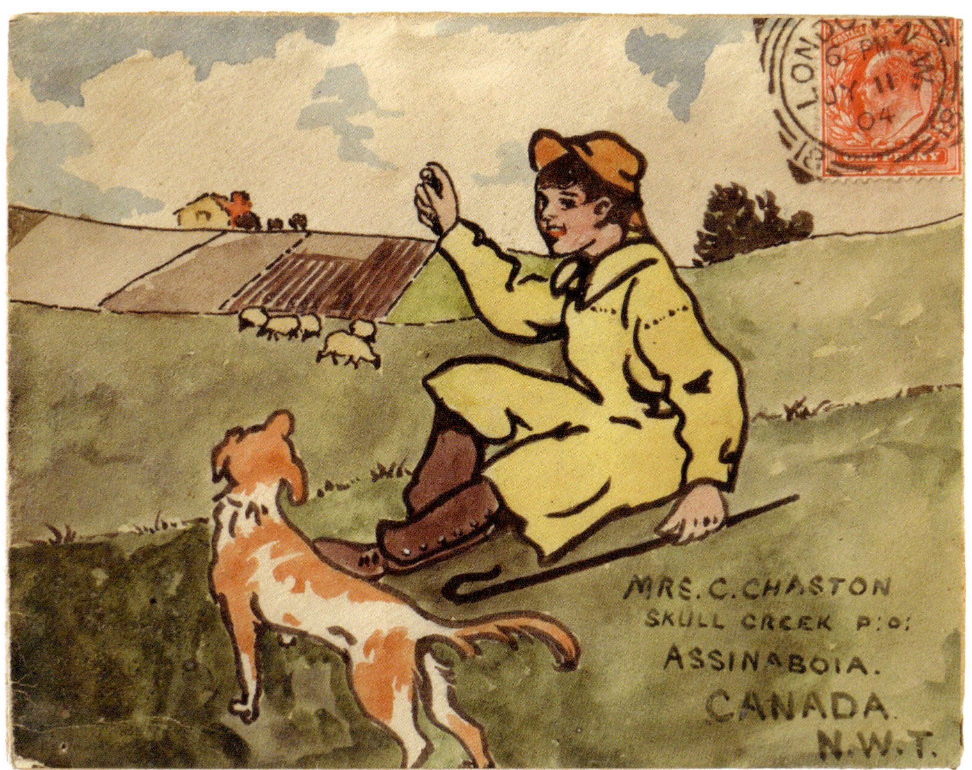

On the return journey we came at one place to a standstill, the trap in water, just up to the floor boards and the horse standing facing a sloping cliff some five feet high. Suddenly the horse takes a gigantic leap upwards and forwards and with a sort of "Tube - lift" feeling inside caused by the sudden jerk, I find myself on dry land trap and all, and the horse trots on quite gaily as though nothing had happened

A long ride in the country

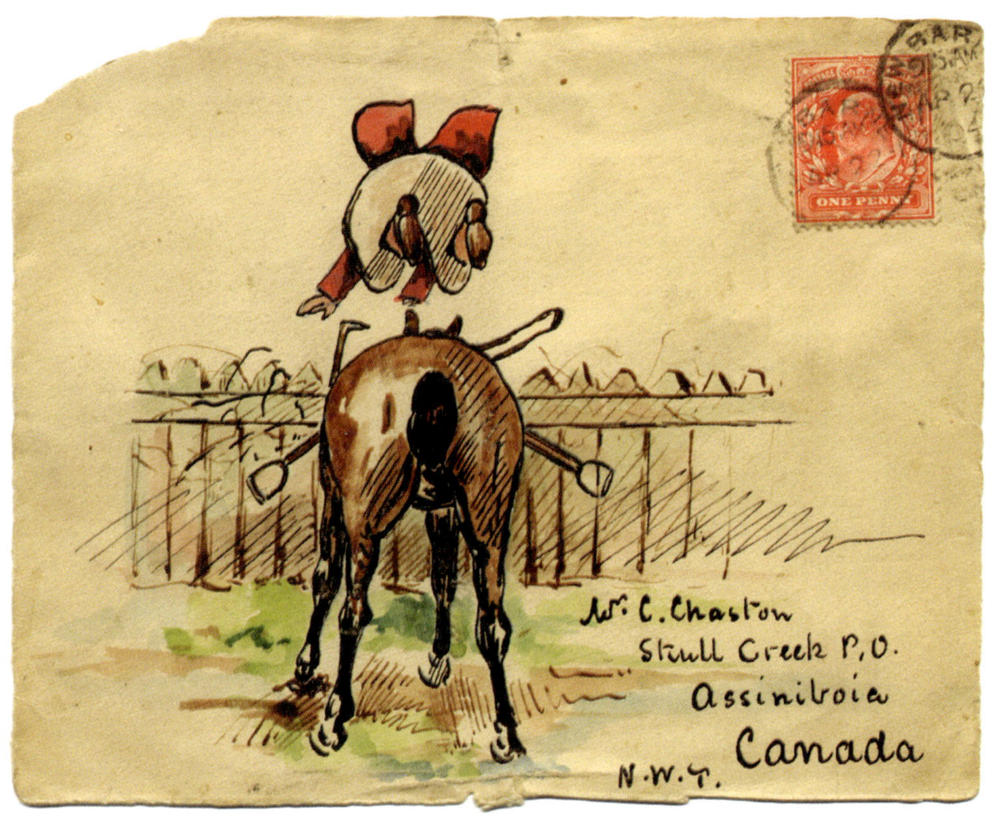

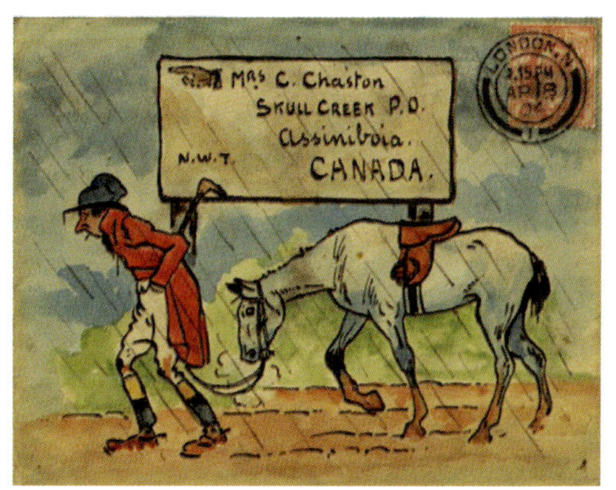
Mrs C. Chaston
Skull Creek P.O.
Assiniboia.
N.W.T.
CANADA.

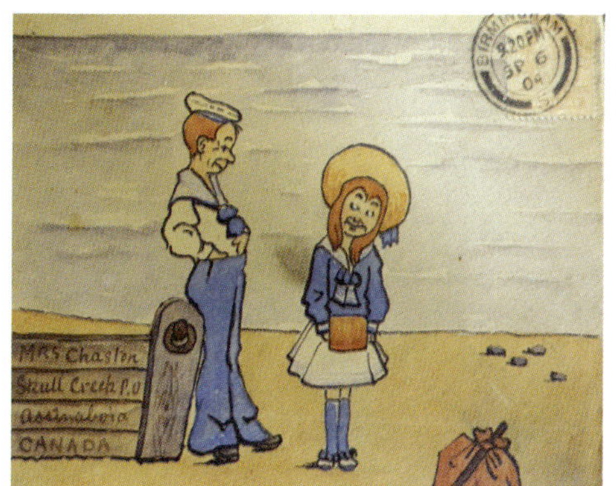
Mrs Chaston
Skull Creek P.O
Assiniboia
CANADA

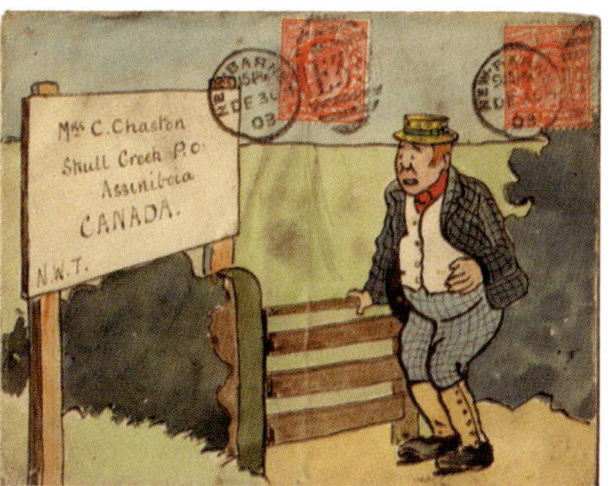
Mrs C. Chaston
Skull Creek P.O.
Assiniboia
CANADA.
N.W.T.

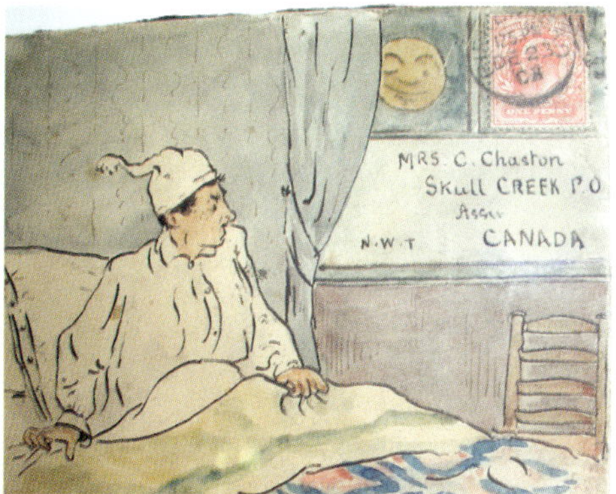
Mrs. C. Chaston
Skull CREEK P.O
Assin
N.W.T.   CANADA

No one should form an opinion of this great country without crossing the Rockies. It is on the west side of these mountains that the most beautiful of things are to be seen, judging by our short tour.

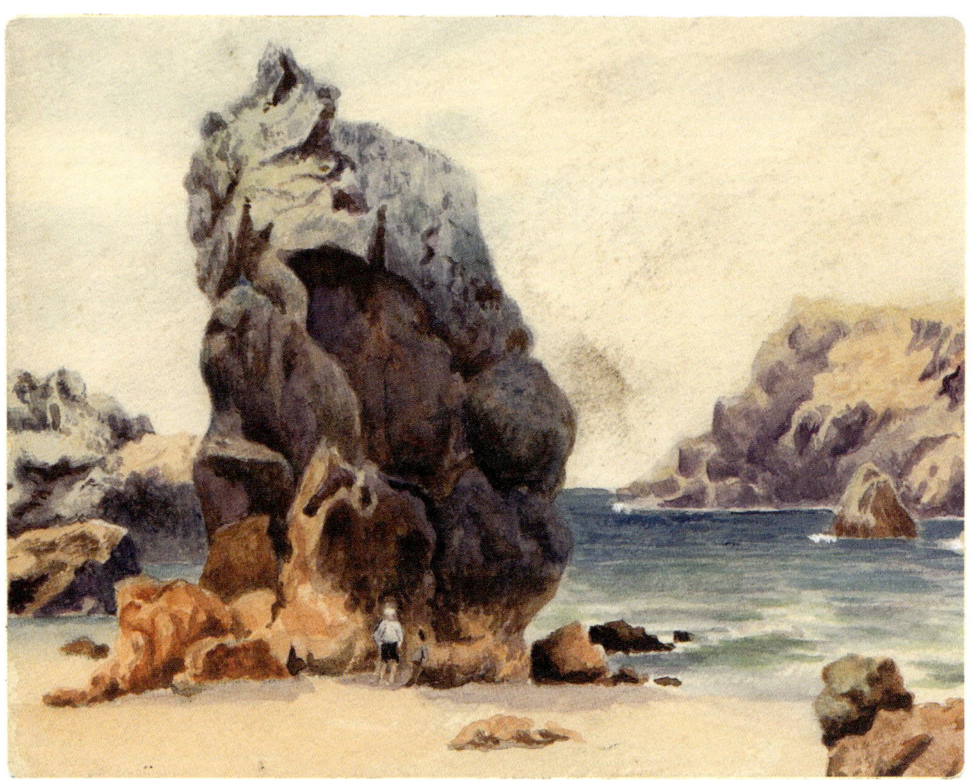

This morning I take a solitary walk along the sea shore, up to Beacon Hill Park, and then to Ross Bay, The cliffs are covered with masses of bright yellow broom, and here and there are clusters of chestnut and maple trees; there are also patches of a tiny blue and white flower that I have never seen before, smelling somewhat like lavender. Eighty or ninety miles away across the sea, are the great snow clad Rocky mountains in the state of Washington; today they are remarkably clear and lovely.

Victoria, 18 May 1911.
No wonder Kittie and her family moved to Victoria fewer than two years later.

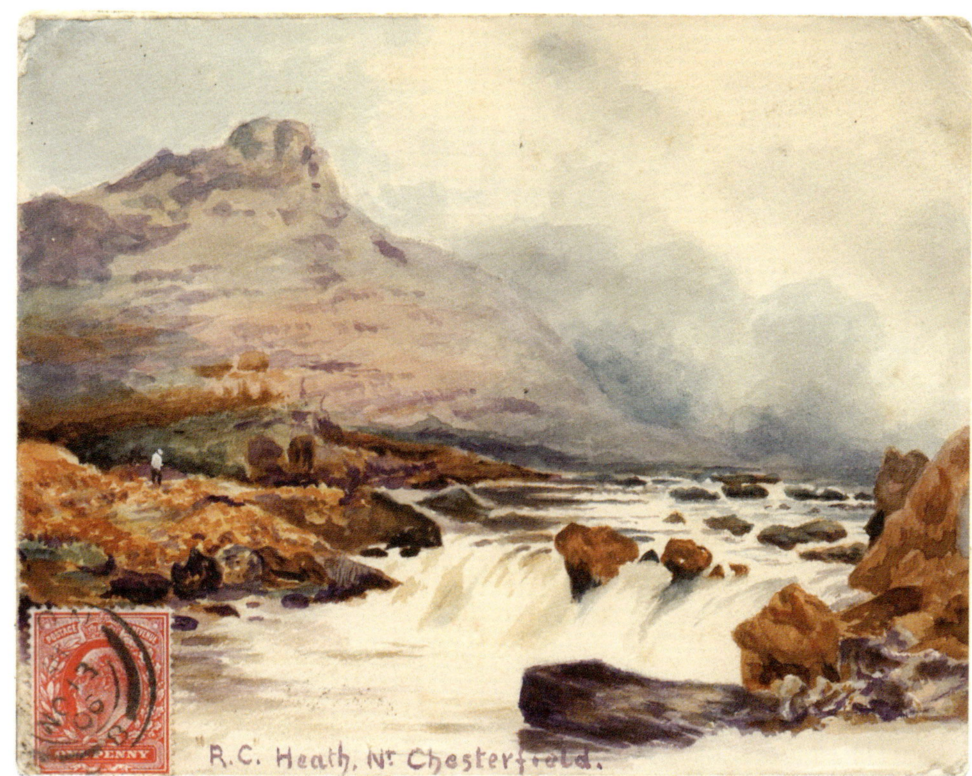

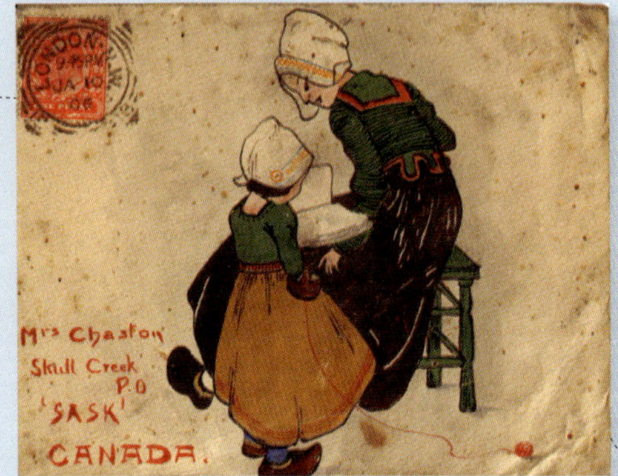

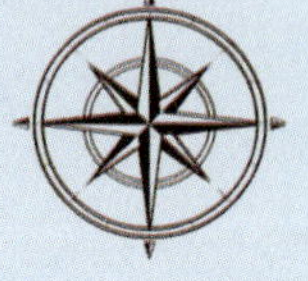

As we have discussed earlier, Harry would from time to time duplicate the design in an envelope, making use of techniques he had learned from his father's printing business. In this case one envelope has been sent to Kittie in Canada and one to Ruth in England. It is not impossible that one went to Isabel in Australia as well.

The one to Kittie has been discoloured from being displayed on a notice board by the Post Master until it was collected.

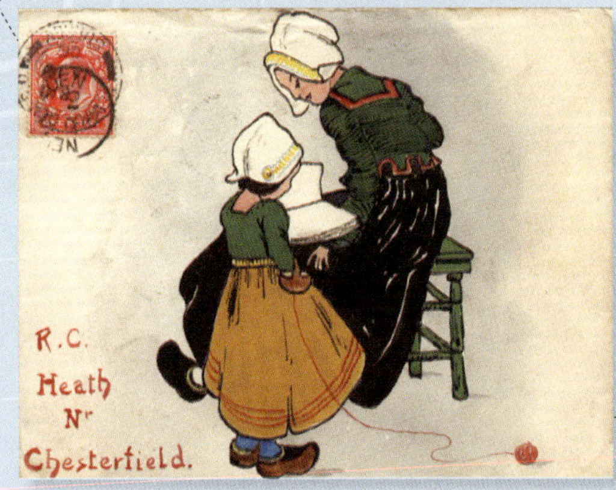

The Sheffield Choir left Victoria on 19 May on board the Zeelandia en route for Australia. There were stops in Hawaii and Fiji before they arrived at Brisbane on 10 June

The Fijians strike me at first glance as being an unusually quiet race. They stand still and without any demonstration just offer you their coral or beads, and if you take no notice of them, they withdraw without a word. The Post Office does a roaring trade for an hour or so, and literally thousands of letters and cards are posted, to say nothing of the purchasing of stamps for the collectors at home. I post 150 items, the contributions of six members of the choir to the English mail.

*A brief stop at Suva, Fiji
Monday June 5th. 1911*

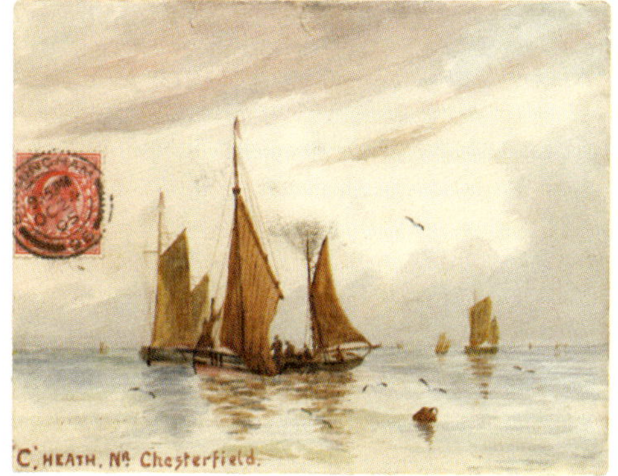

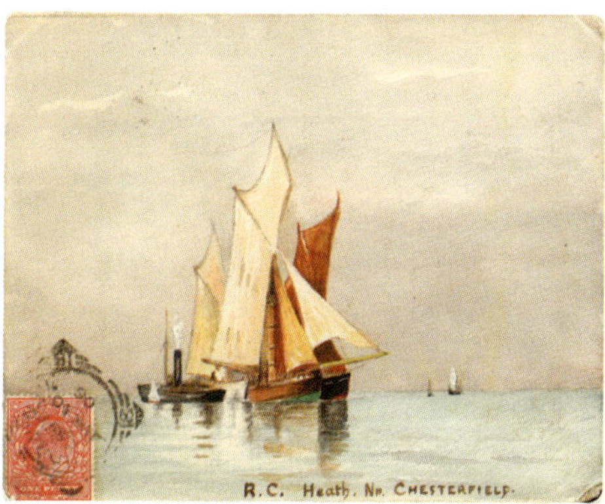

Isabel,
Gawler, Australia

AUSTRALIA
Isabel, Gawler

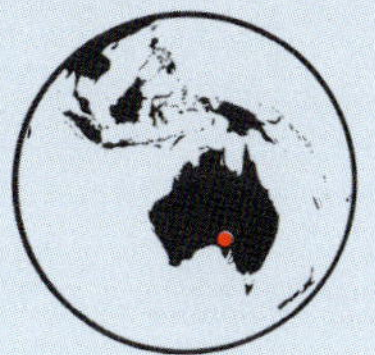

Our last day at sea. I am wildly excited at the prospect of seeing Australia, having had so much correspondence with the place (writing to Arthur and Isabel) during the past twenty-two years.

Phil's diary 9 June 1911

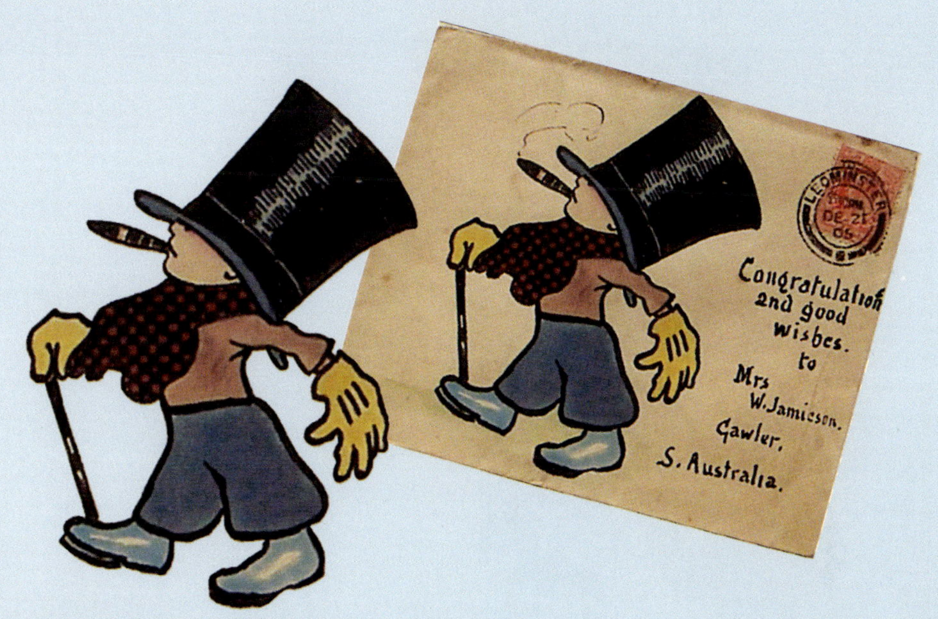

We all troop on board the "Lucinda", a little river steamer which takes us up the 10 or 12 miles to Brisbane. The "Lucinda" brings our English letters, the first we have had for nearly four weeks, and we are all too fully occupied in reading home news to notice the pretty river scenery or the friendly welcomes that are waved to us from almost every villa. Arriving at Kennedy Wharf, trams are in readiness to take us to the Botanical Gardens, the streets being more or less lined with interested spectators. Passing the Post Office, I drop off the tram and send a telegram to Melbourne, announcing my safe arrival on Australian shores.

While in Sydney I join the party going to La Perouse and Botany Bay...The tram runs along its own special road way, right across a lovely common or scrub, where the bushes cover the land, and grow quite close together.

La Perouse, is the 'original' name of Australia, and it is also the name of a little village or reserve inhabited by a few Aboriginals; they live in little wooden houses, prettily dotted about on the sandy hills, close to the waters of the bay. . . .

Phil arriving in Sydney
12 June 1911

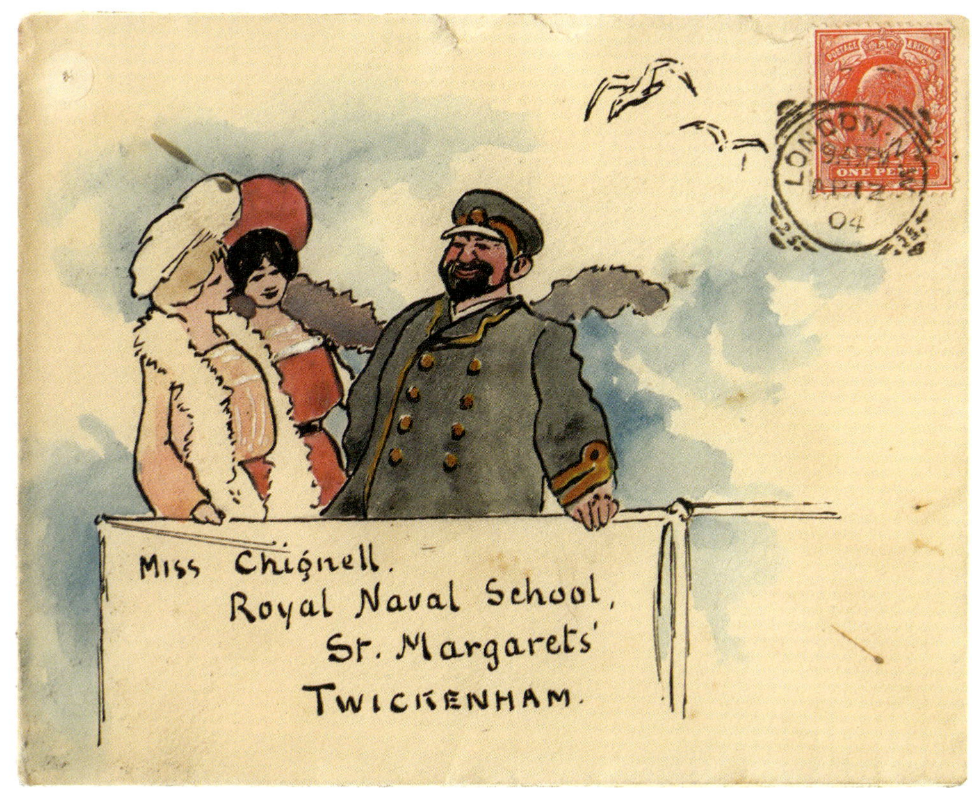

Next comes "Grannie", my own Mother, not changed in the least, since I last saw her, three years ago. Three years is a mere nothing in the history of our family, where we sometimes count years of absence by tens and dozens.

Phil on seeing his family, Melbourne.

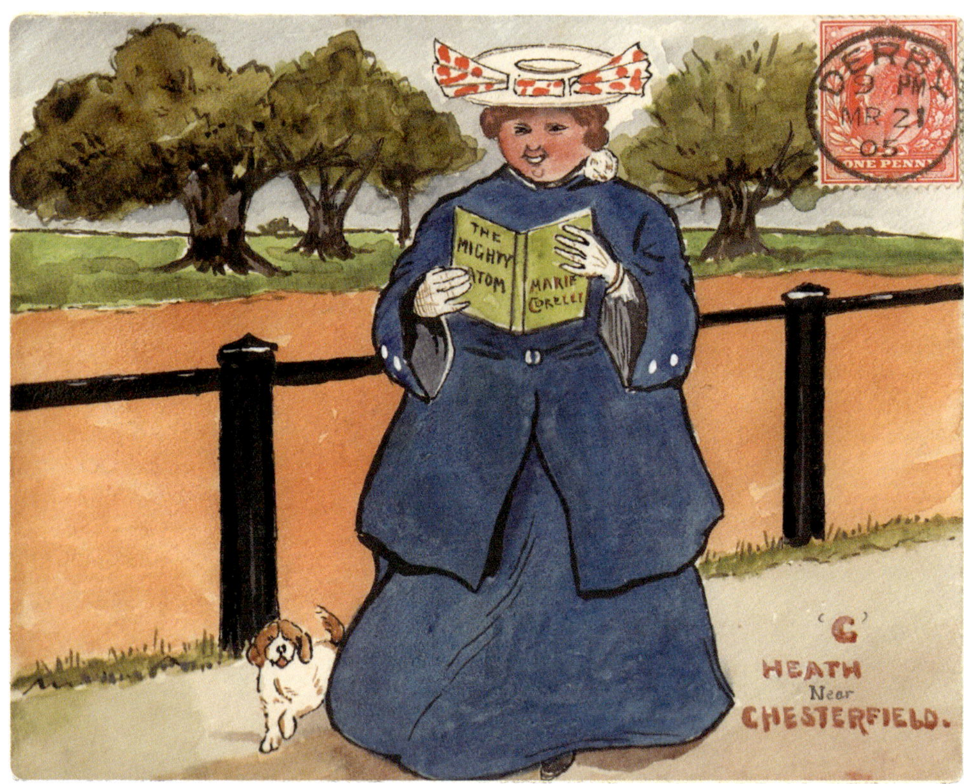

Outside the church a steep decline brings me to Gawler River, where I find a very pretty walk, along the twisting river bank, under the pepper and gum trees, the former, especially, being very dainty and sweet.
In the neighbouring gardens are almond trees in full blossom, and orange and lemon trees with fruit hanging plentifully from the branches. Altogether I am very pleasantly surprised at the sweetness of the place.

Phil visits Gawler, twenty-five miles north of Adelaide where Isabel had lived until recently.

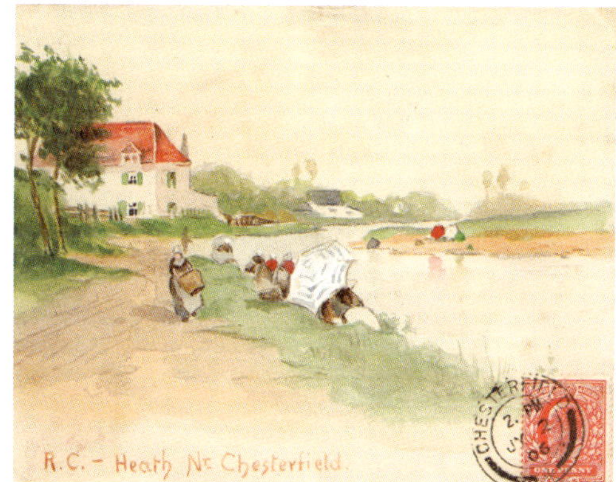

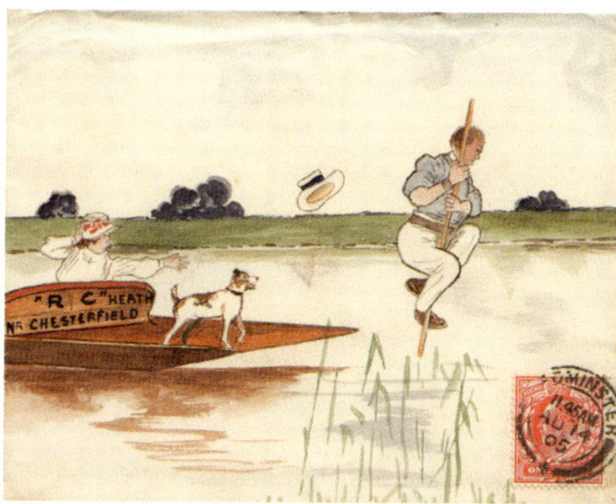

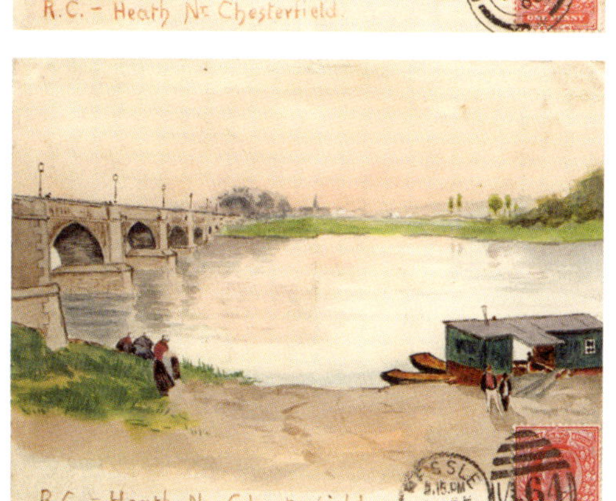

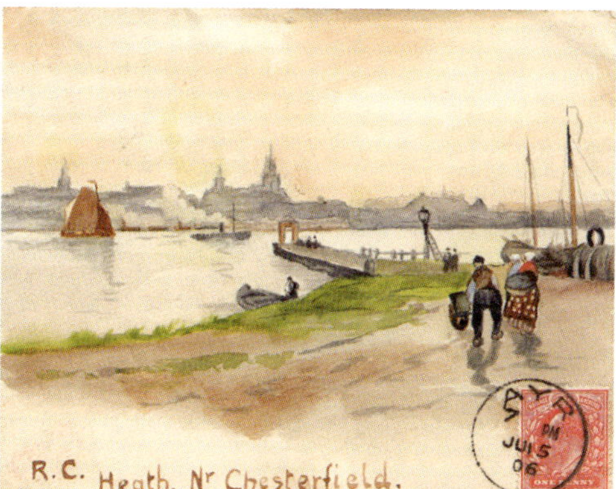

Many partly interesting novelties to me, for although the larks' songs remind me of England, there are magpies, laughing jackasses, and minahs, to keep me amused. Of trees, the silver wattle is in full bloom, looking almost more glorious and laburnum in an English June; in many places it gives the roadside a touch of brilliancy beyond any thing yet seen outside the tropics. The Australian gum tree is never absent from the scene, and its peculiarity is that it grows best in isolation; on many a sloping hillside can be seen just one of these trees, looking dainty and perhaps a little desolate, all by itself. It has very little foliage considering the size, and this gives it a delicate appearance.

Phil on a walk with with Isabel's husband in Melbourne on 19 June.

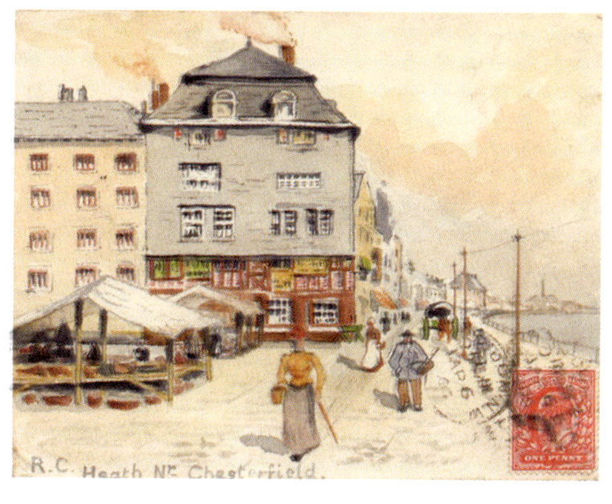

R.C. Heath Nr Chesterfield.

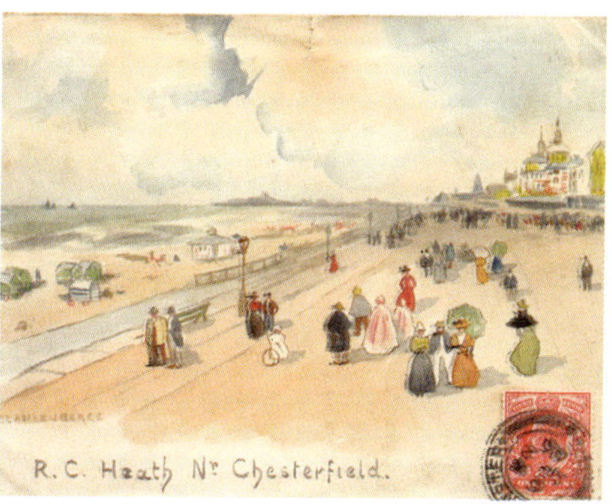

R.C. Heath Nr Chesterfield.

Arthur was in England when I left, he said "good bye" to me at Liverpool, intending to meet me again at Sydney, but his time-table went wrong, and when I was just leaving Sydney [where he had received his copy of *An Outpost in Papua*] for Auckland, he was just arriving at Melbourne, and he actually reached Sydney three days after I had left.

When I was at Sydney, he was at Melbourne, and now that I am at Melbourne, he is at Brisbane. He is now returning to his work in the Papuan Mission, after a year's holiday.

Phil's diary on missing Arthur

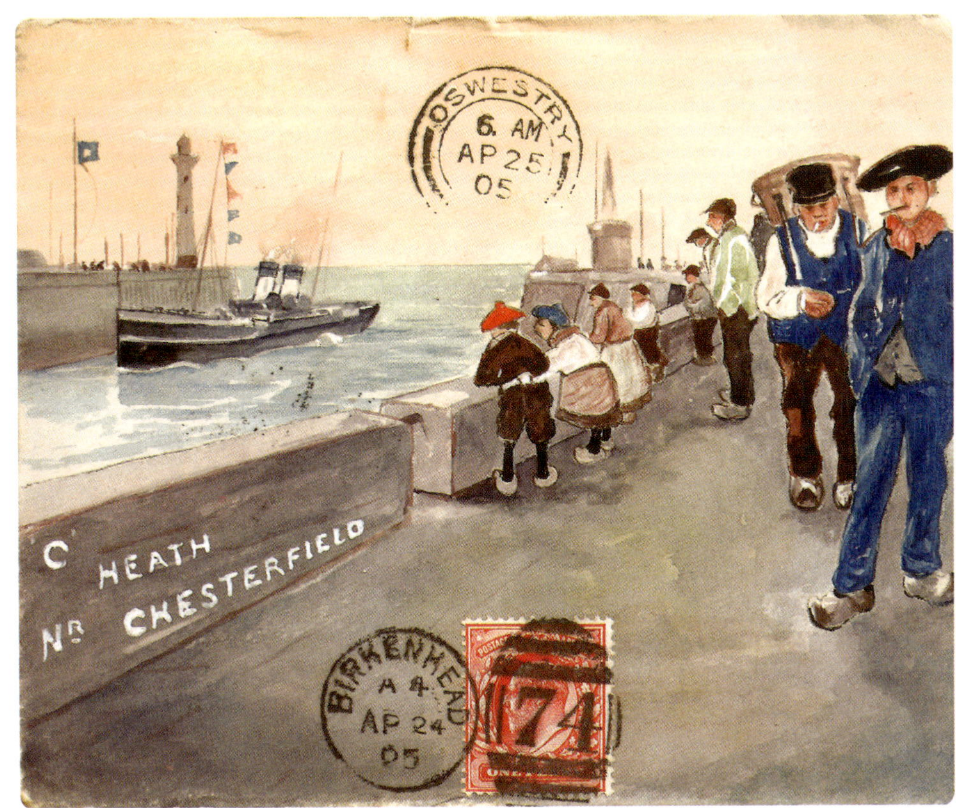

We part, with no knowledge of the future, or if we shall ever meet again. With Mother it is different, for I hope to see her in England next April, and I have said so many long "good byes" to her during the last few years, that I am hardened, more or less.

Phil leaving Melbourne on 23 July

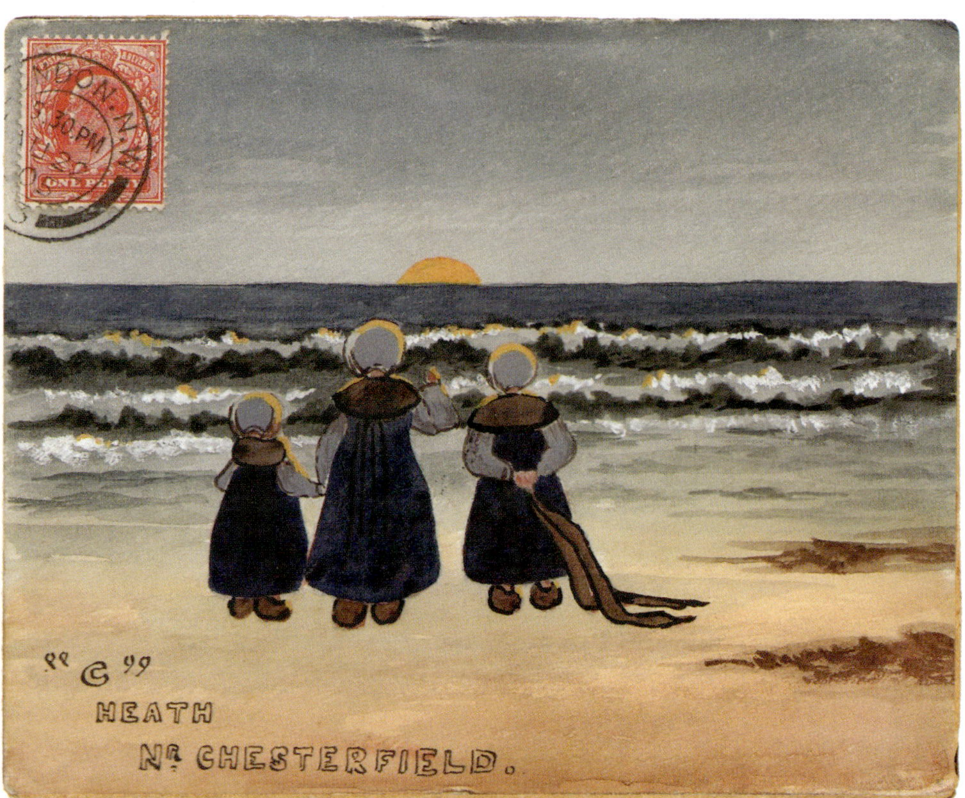

Arthur,
Papua New Guinea

PAPUA
Arthur, Wanigera

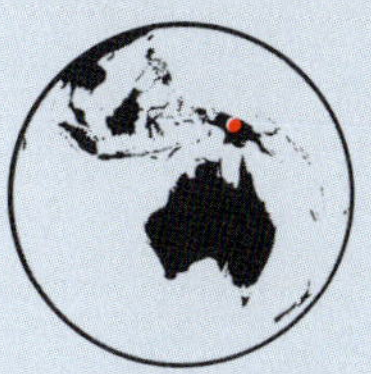

In 1907 Arthur moved to Papua where he was a missionary. While in Papua he took field notes about the local customs. These were included in *An Outpost in Papua*.

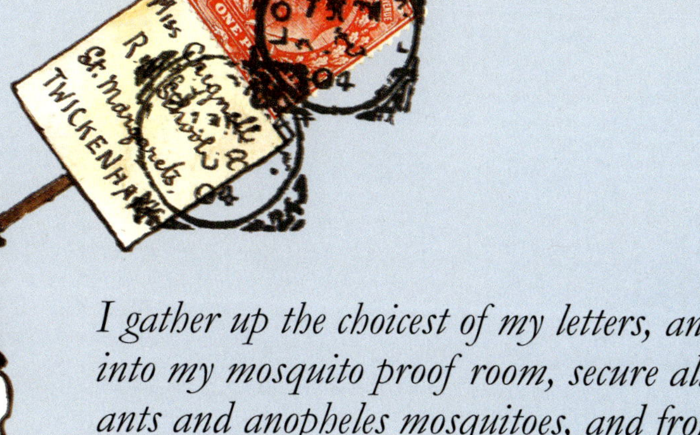

I gather up the choicest of my letters, and go with them into my mosquito proof room, secure alike from flying ants and anopheles mosquitoes, and from any imminent probability of human interruption, and lose myself, completely, for a little while, in the wider world that is not so very far away from Wanigera after all.

An Outpost in Papua

When we arrived that first time in Wanigera... the night was black, with no moon and never a star to guide us, and though the deep sea-water was marked with phosphorescent streaks where fish moved beneath us, and the oars sparkled and left swirling patches of of liquid fire in the places where they had been dipped, and the wake of our whalesboat, as we came from Uiaku, shone dimly luminous far behind us, the shore was dark and no landmark could be seen, except a small red fire under a house in the mid-way village of Yuayu.

Arthur's first view of his new home in Papua.
From *An Outpost in Papua*

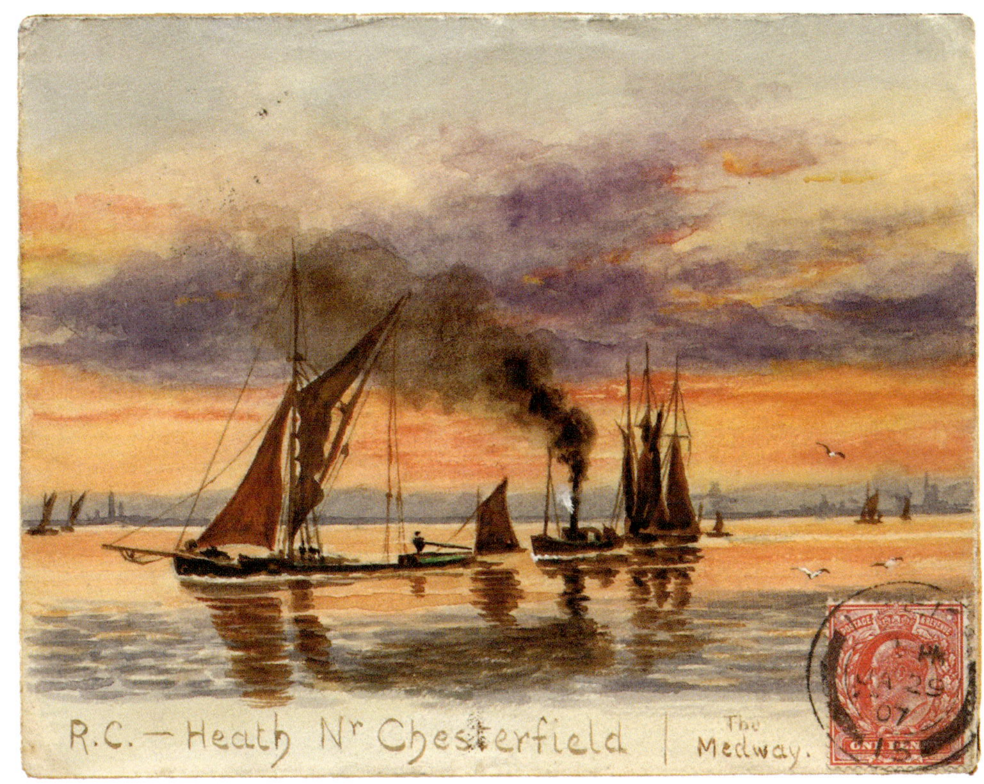

It is not every man who can boast of an active volcano in his backyard, but there it is eight or ten miles behind my station, red and gold in the early morning, and purple or grey towards evening, always with white steam, or spirals of darker smoke ascending from a dozen fizzures in its rugged crown. The elder men in Wanigera will tell you of a time when 'the burning mountain' burst asunder, and sent flaming streams of lava flowing down to the sea.

Arthur settles in.
From *An Outpost in Papua.*

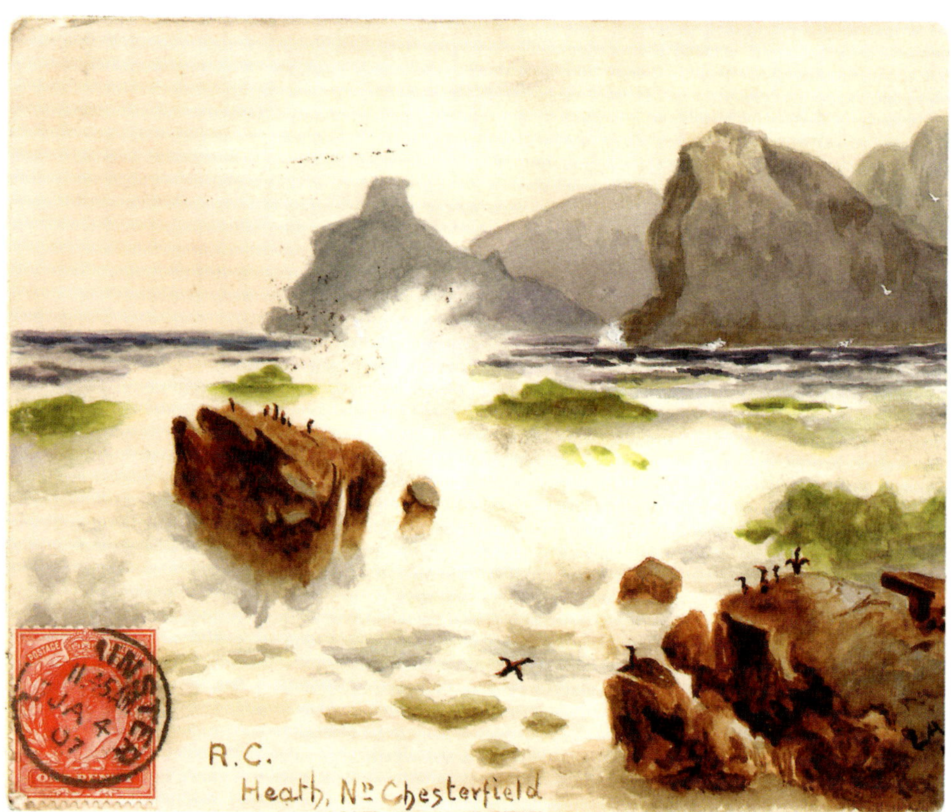

Arthur gathered a number of
artifacts and sent them to his
father in England who in turn
sold them to the Pitt Rivers
Museum in Oxford where they
still remain.

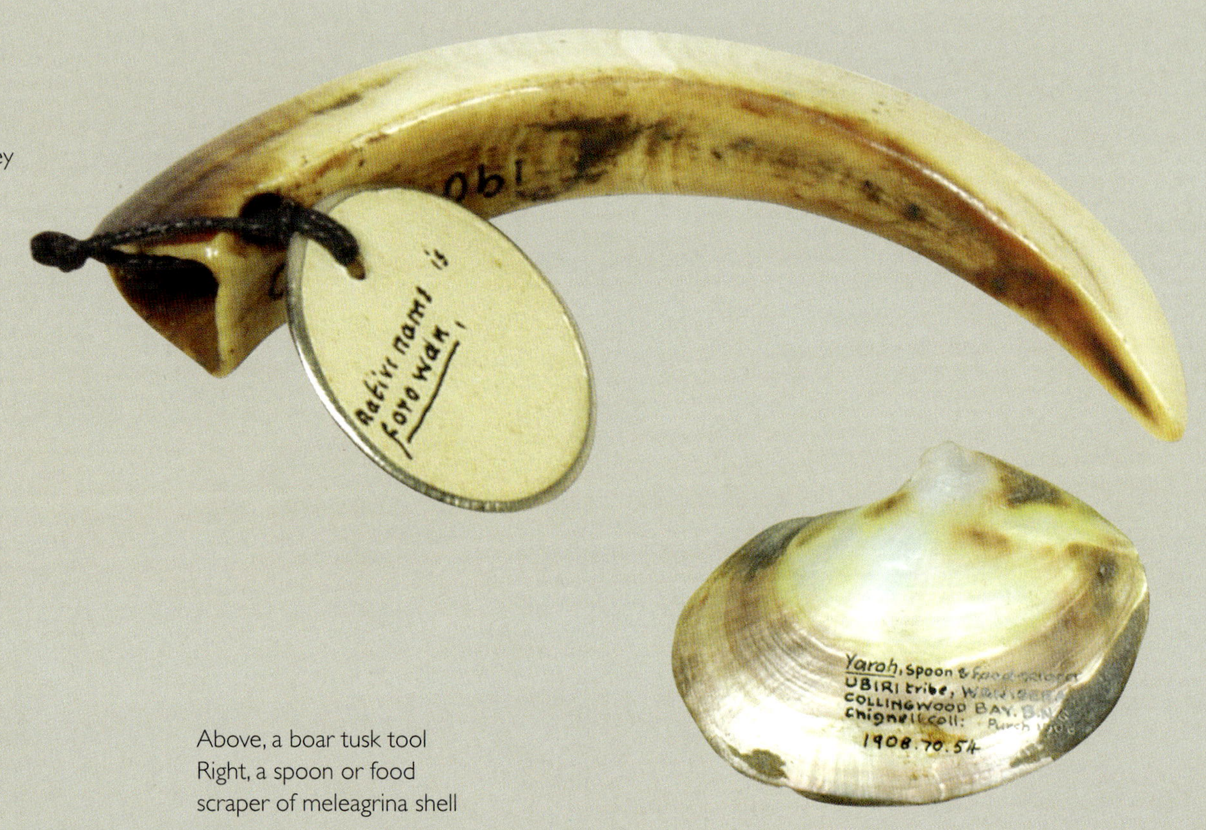

Above, a boar tusk tool
Right, a spoon or food
scraper of meleagrina shell

Below, ear ornament of a ring of
coconut shell with halved coix seeds
bound around the edge and with
pendant strings

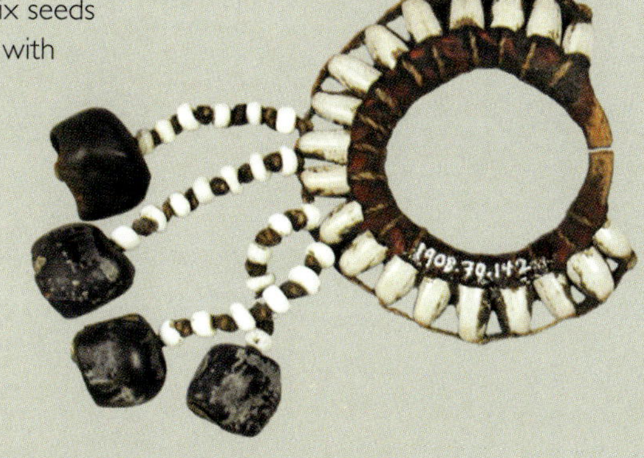

*You would think that they surely been made at the same time,
by the same hands. And yet the one was used as a razor two
thousand years ago in my own country ... and the other was
made and used for an exactly similar purpose quite lately here
in Wanigera by some Papuan who was fain to shave himself...*

Comparing a 'strangely shaped piece of flint' Arthur found years ago
in Suffolk and an object he acquired in Papua — a razor made of obsidian

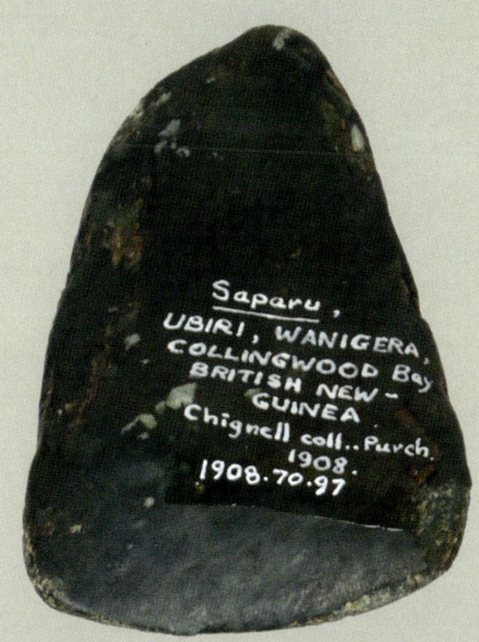

No one had prepared me for the ordered beauty of the place... with a frontage of a hundred yards eastward to the sea... hedges of carefully-pruned lime-trees... clumps of bright, green-leaved hibiscus, with flaming scarlet flowers; and row upon row of native houses coming close up to the station fence on either hand.

Arthur's impressions.
From *An Outpost in Papua.*

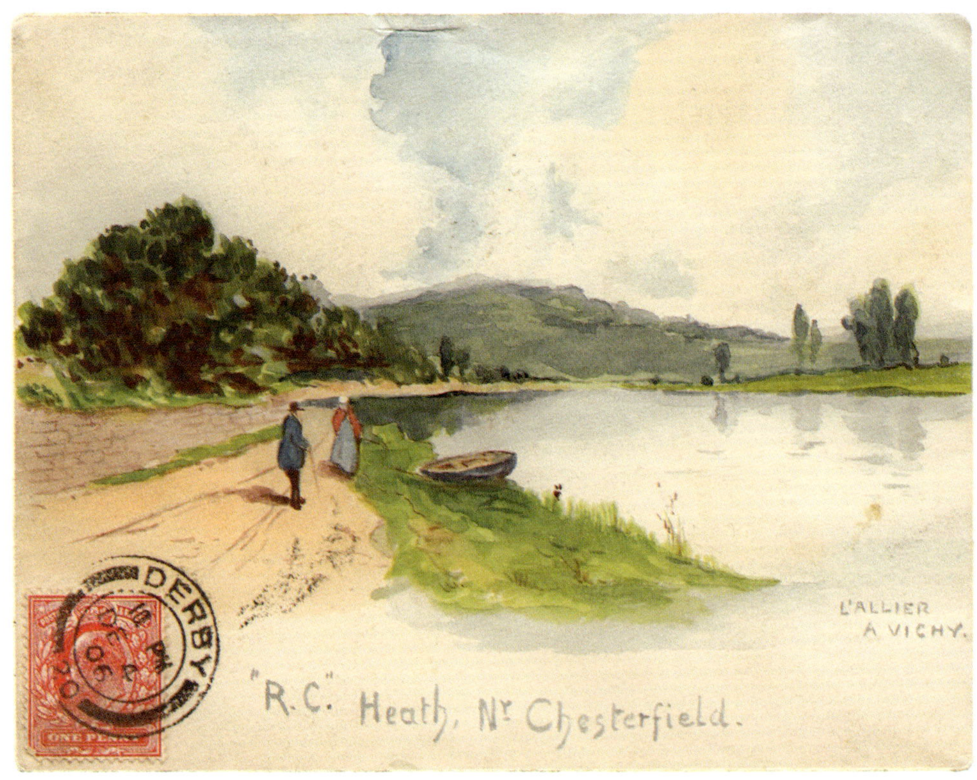

*Certain seasons are appointed for different kinds of work —
the hollowing out of canoes, the making of nets, the building and
repairing of houses, the shaping of paddles and sharpening
spears, the making of pots and native cloth, getting and preparing
of sago, the clearing off of land for gardens — Certain seasons
for fishing and hunting, and for making ventures along
the coast for trade with other tribes. But there is almost no idleness.*

Life as Arthur described it in *An Outpost in Papua.*

We miss him for he was a good launch captain and we on the out-stations miss the sudden surprises of his comings and the wonderful mails, only a day and a half from Samarai, which means that the English letters and mails were no more than two months old, and those from Australia often even less than a month.

On the death of the captain.
From *An Outpost in Papua.*

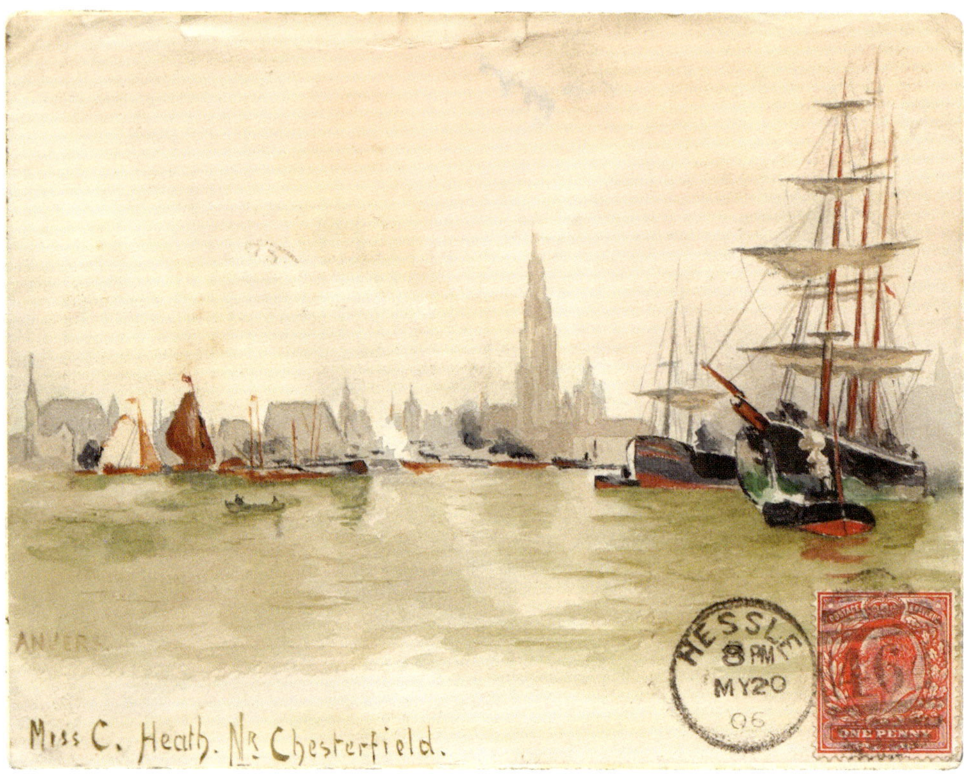

We get letters, and answer them, but there are no particular or precise means....Letters come at random, anyhow and anywhere.... A year or so ago, at three o'clock one afternoon, just as it was beginning to rain, a small cutter came round Keppel Point, and made for the anchorage behind the reef... A couple of shots were fired from the cutter as she anchored, and our whale boat was at once sent out to her... the splendid unexpectedness of everything that happens here— an unexpectedness which is never more noticeable, to some of us, than where our letters are concerned.

An Outpost in Papua, p. 246, 248

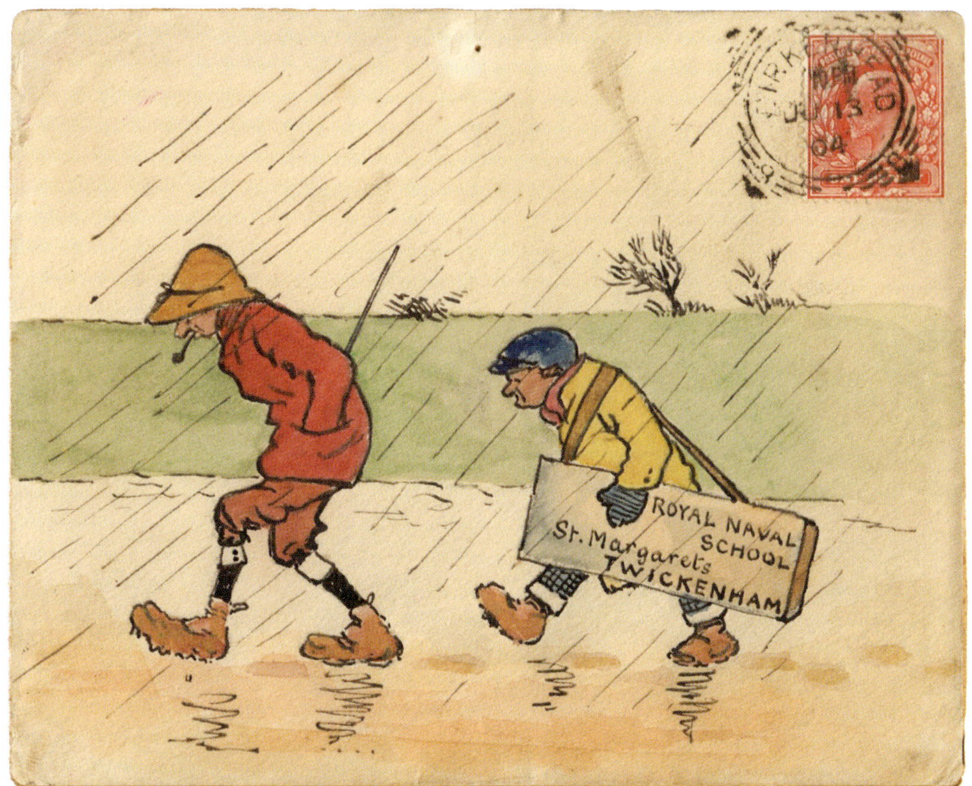

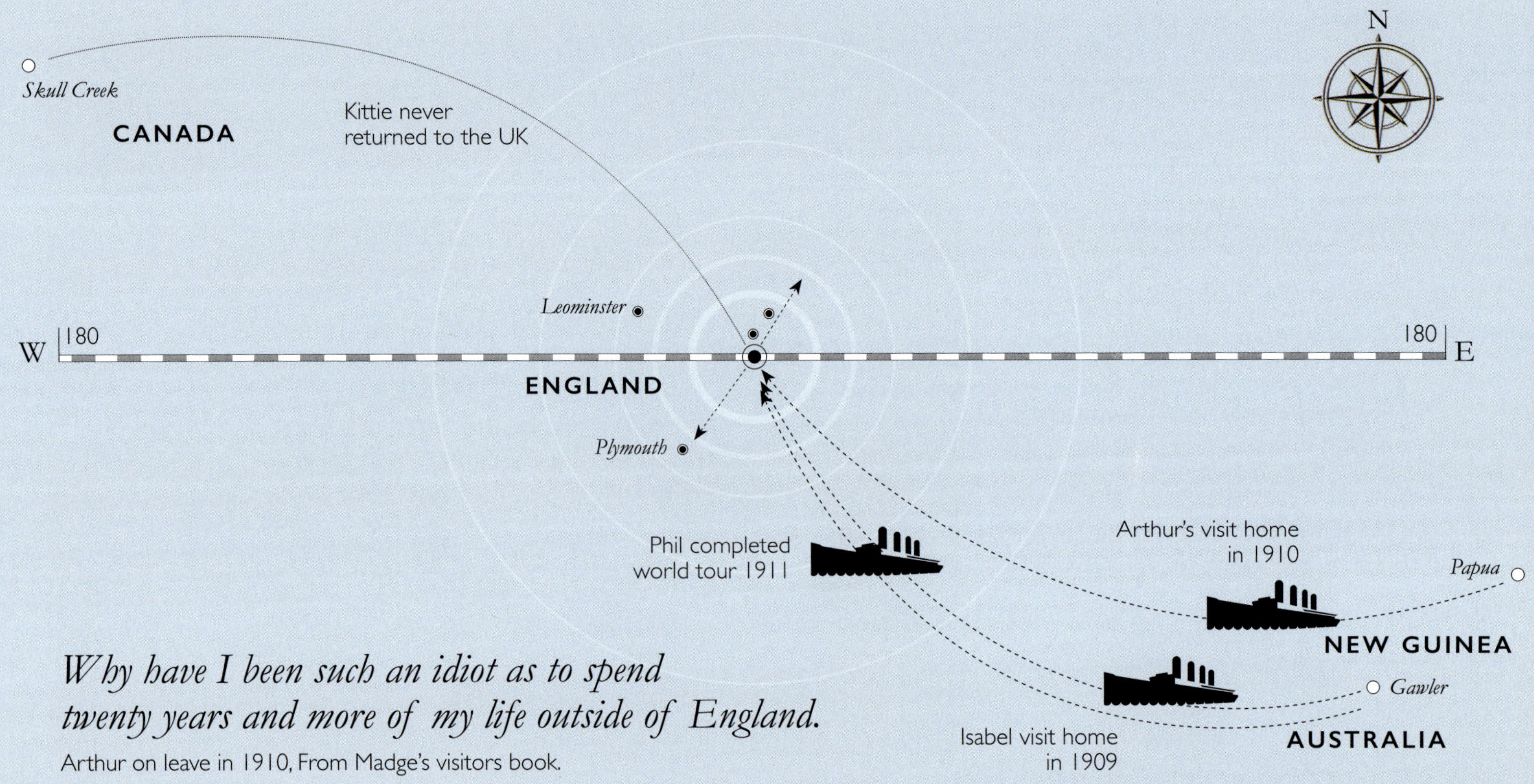

Why have I been such an idiot as to spend twenty years and more of my life outside of England.

Arthur on leave in 1910, From Madge's visitors book.

Came straight here from Rondebosch, and the shadow of Table Mountain, South Africa. How's that for a record? It is lovely to be back again in cool, breezy old England, after a trip of 38,000 miles.

Phil's entry in Madge's visitors book for Oct 1-3 1911 when he had just returned from his world tour with the Sheffield choir.

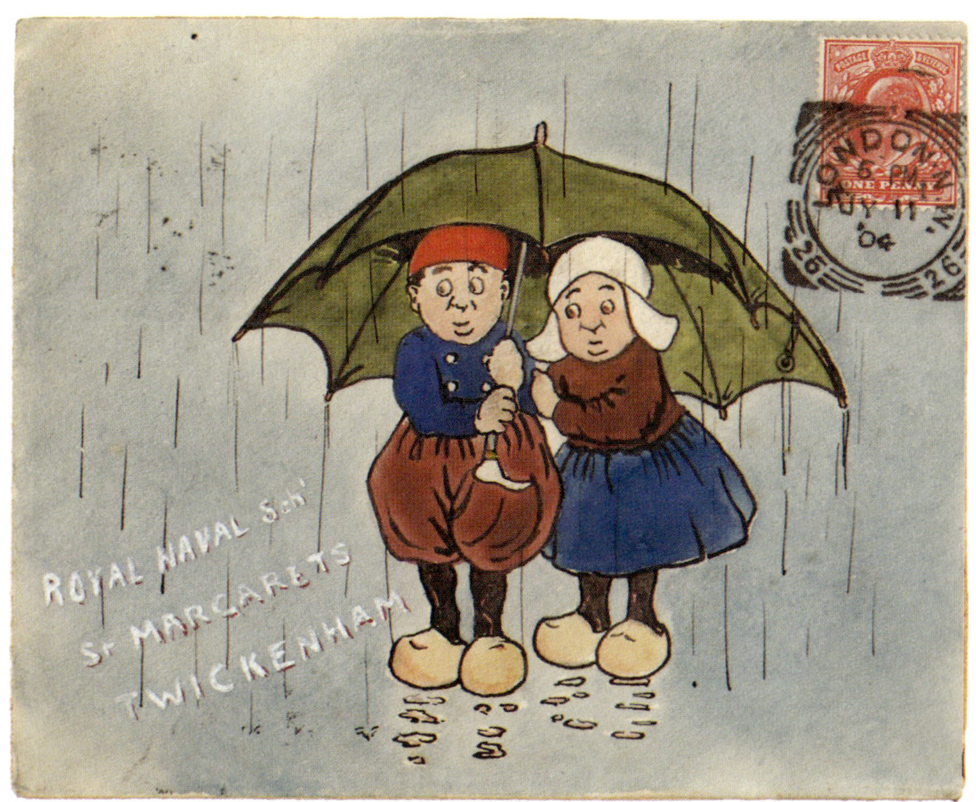

Norman, England

ENGLAND
Home team, Norman

London
Merchant Taylors

Cambridge
Clare College

Jersey

Godalming
Charterhouse school

We had prayers at 9:10. I can still remember it all very clearly: the scurry up the steps to the Great Hall... And then to see Dr Baker come in for a moment and sit on his 'throne'. Then to see him rise and say in a rather high-pitched voice, 'Qui – et Prayers'

Norman, the youngest of the children, started as a day boy at Merchant Taylors School in London, September 1893

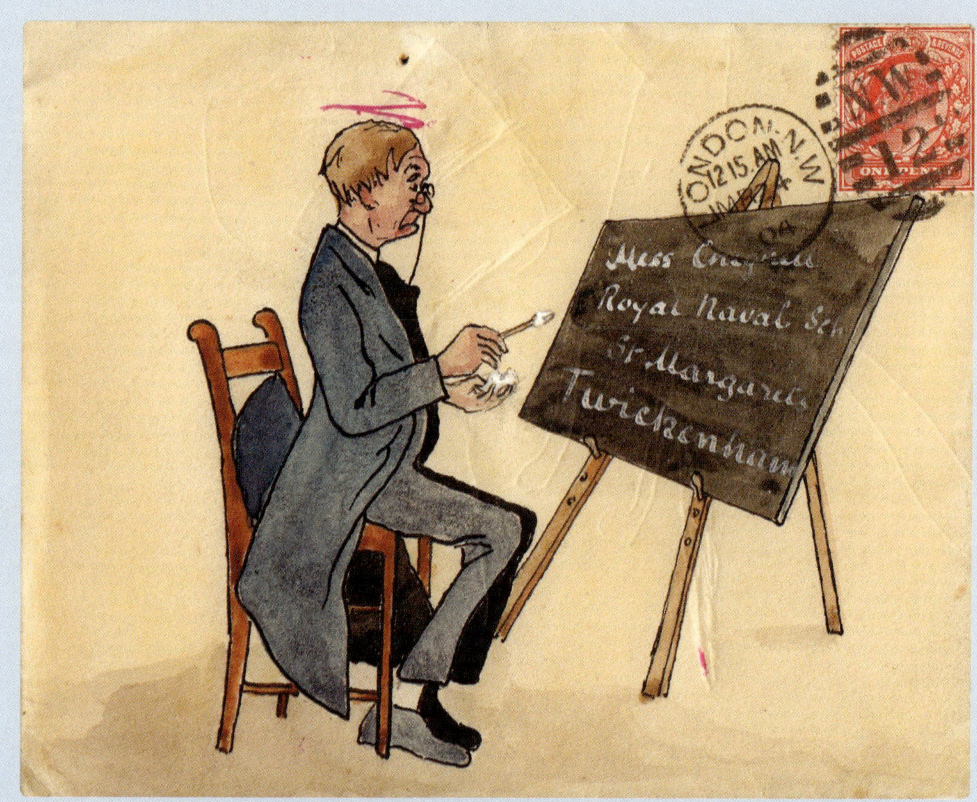

An hour or so later I was travelling back to London on one of those beautiful days we sometimes get in the middle of winter and my train dashing through the flat eastern counties with windmills turning and flashing in the sun, and I remember feeling how unreal it all was – how the world had almost come to an end because an old woman had died'.

Norman returning to school after Queen Victoria's death on Jan 22, 1901

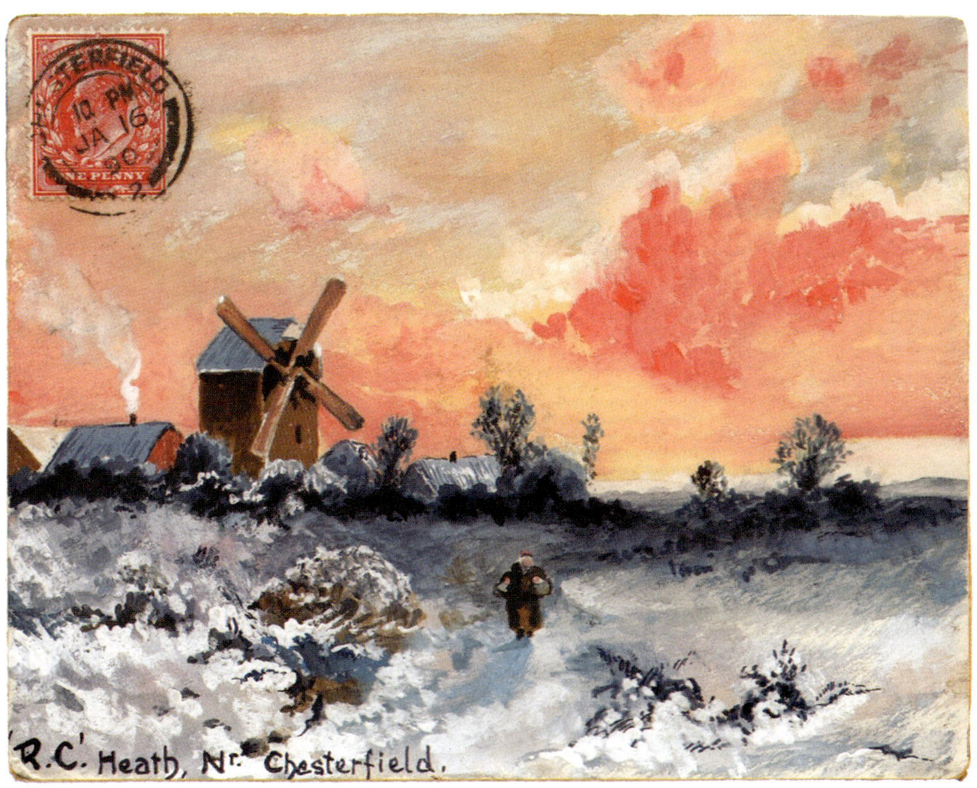

I did not have rooms in College my first year but lodged with an old harridan of a landlady named Mrs Jones and waited on by a quite impossible maid.

*Norman in his first year at
Clare College, Cambridge*

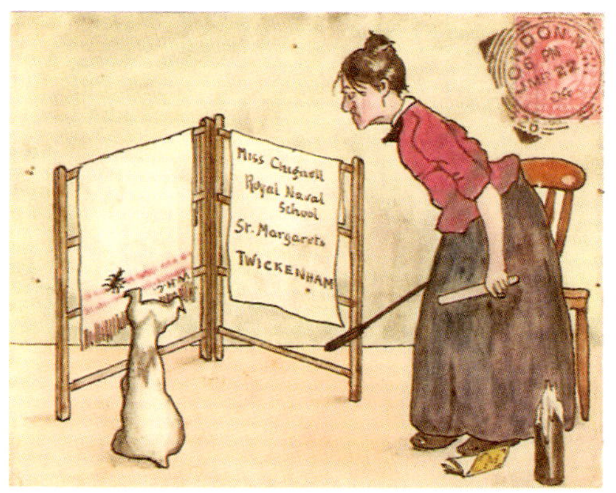

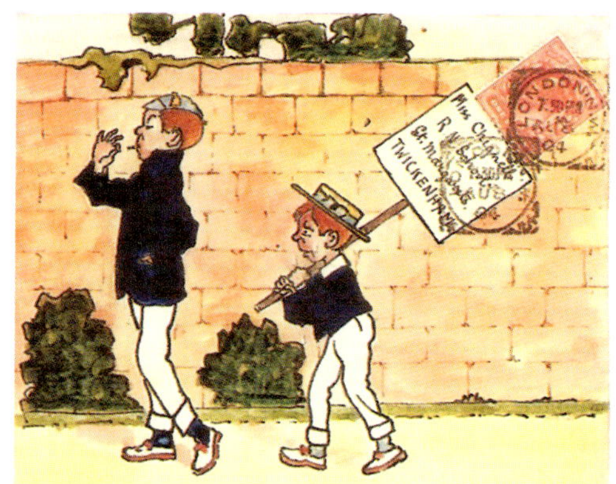

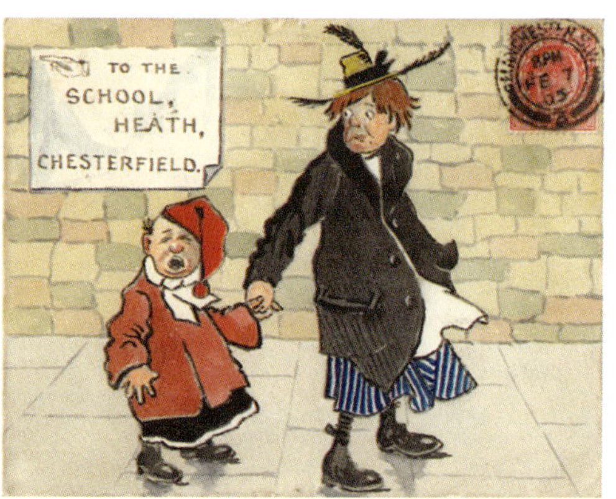

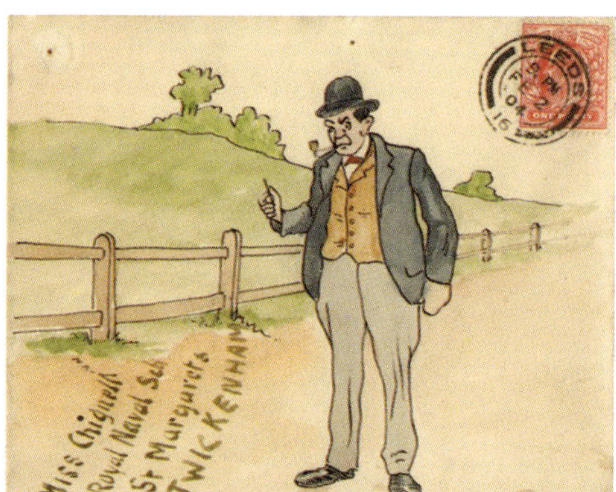

J. H. Grace was brilliant in the realm of mathematics. He never at any time referred to text books or notes, but would just sit down and talk and talk, and would present the most complicated details of some of the more elaborate parts of higher mathematics just straight from his own brain, at express speed and with compelling lucidity.

Norman at Clare College.
J.H. Grace was his mathematics tutor

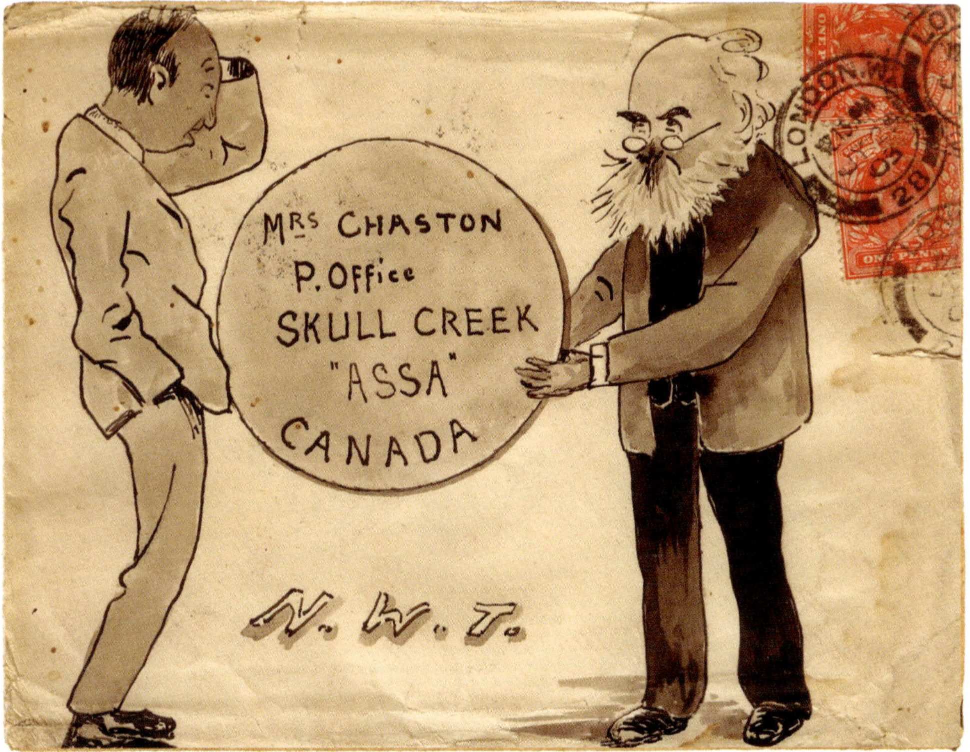

Clement Durrell was a Scholar of Clare, a year senior to myself. He lived at Fulbourn and had a large family of sisters, none of them married, and I can quite believe that he was encouraged to introduce eligible undergraduates to that family... I used to borrow a bicycle to ride over there in the afternoon for tea and a bit of flirtation.

Durrell would later become the author of several important books on algebra.

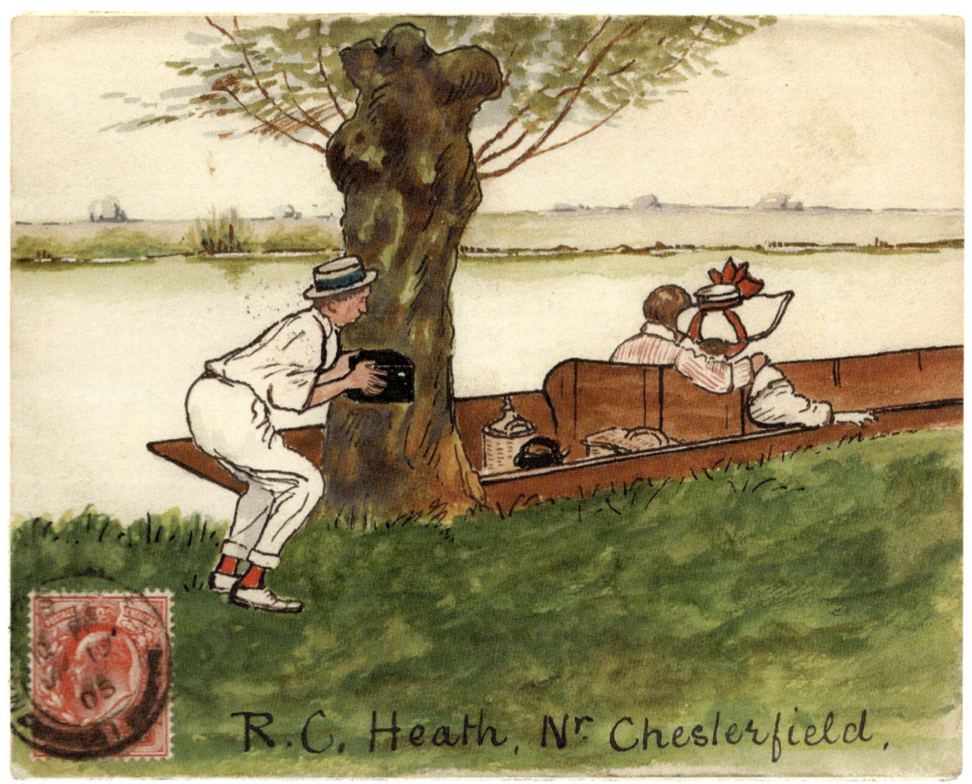

Jersey was an exceedingly pleasant place in which to start a career. The living itself was cheap and good – luxuries like lobster were well within the means of even my slender purse. There was no Income Tax and there was plenty of sun and fresh air.

Norman's first teaching job was at Victoria College in Jersey 1905.

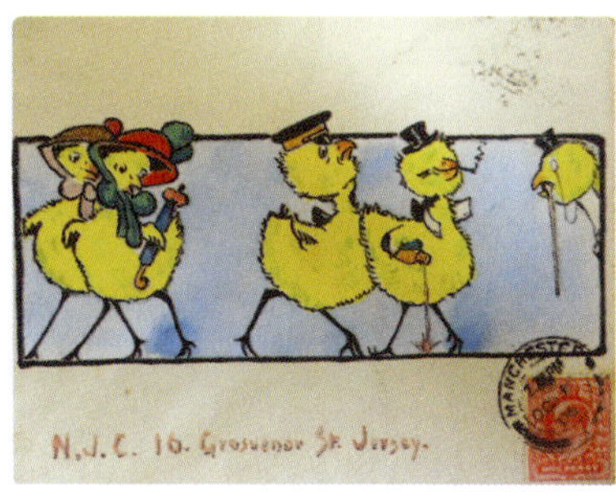

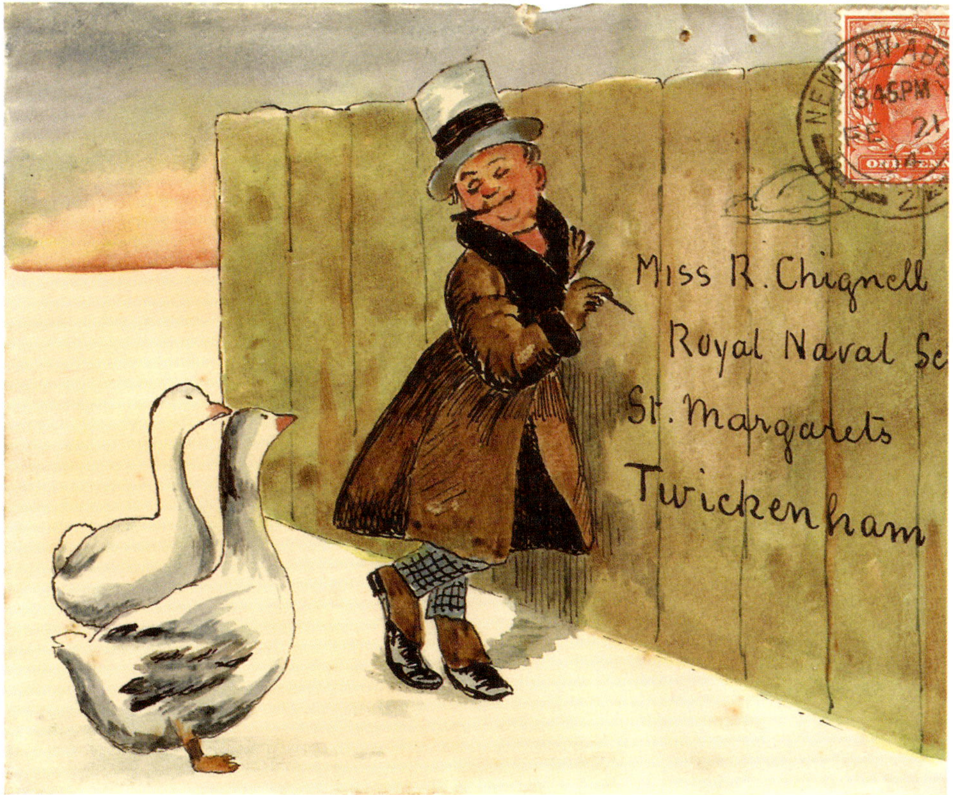

I bought my first bicycle when I went to Jersey and during my two years there I covered most of the paths on the island. It was long before there had been any proper roads on the Island and all the roads were literally just country roads.

I don't think any of them had been tarred and at the time of potato digging they got pretty dirty with all the traffic.

Life in Jersey in the first decade of the twentieth century.

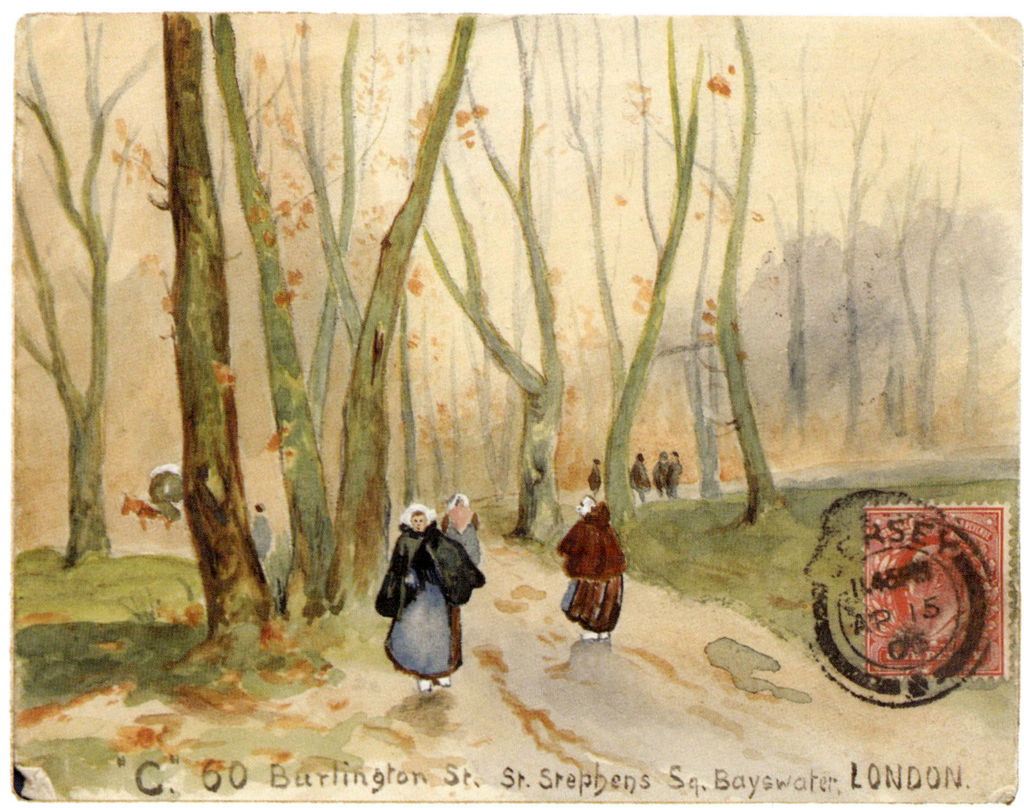

I shall never forget Isabel's joy
at the journey. The woods were full
of primroses, and Isabel fresh
from the comparative hardness
of Australia, almost wept at this sight
and said that she simply must
stop the train and get out and
pick all those primroses "before
the other children get them".

On 14 April 1909 Norman arrived at
Plymouth to greet Isabel's ship.
The next morning they took a train
back to Leominster.

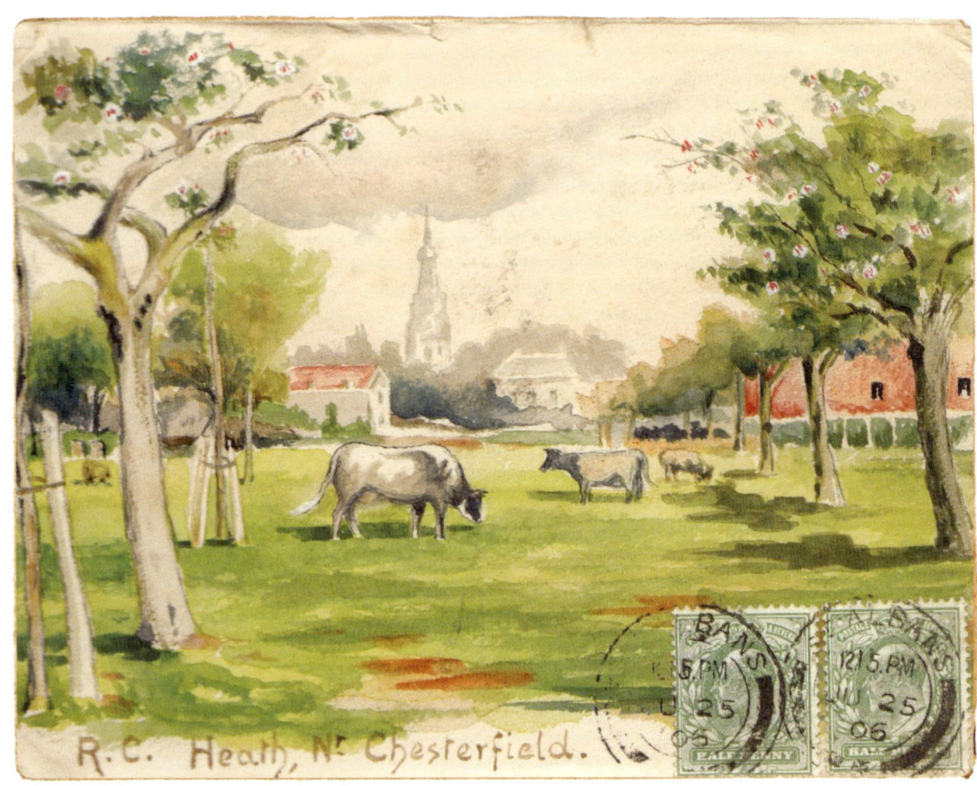

Isabel was, of course, the heroine of the occasion and I remember many gentle walks I had with her – one always referred to in later years as 'the little green door' when we wandered down the road and found a door in a wall, and something tempted us to open it up and go through, and we had a queer sentimental sense of having walked into paradise. I don't suppose there was anything very startling about it but Isabel had a romantic nature and the sense of adventure was strong on us.

Norman's description of the holiday the siblings took to St Arvans in Wales later that summer.

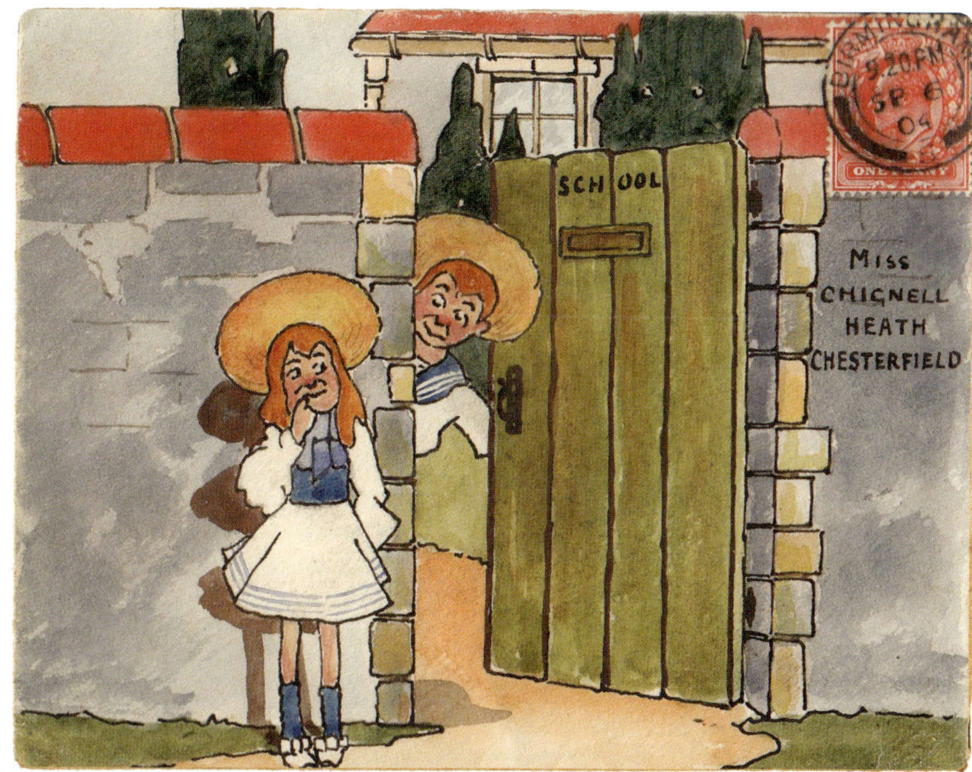

And then one day Phil and I went off for a long walk, leaving Madge, Isabel and Ruth lazing about in the cottage in St Arvans. We came back to find them playing "magic" – it may have been Planchette, or it may have been with an inverted tumbler, but it sticks in my mind that we challenged Ruth (who seemed to be the clairvoyant of the party) to tell us by her spirit reading, or whatever it might be, where we had had tea. I can't believe it at this distance of years but I think she did actually produce the name of the obscure village where we had been – and she had no means whatever of having gained the knowledge by any independent means.

Norman's continued description of the Welsh holiday.

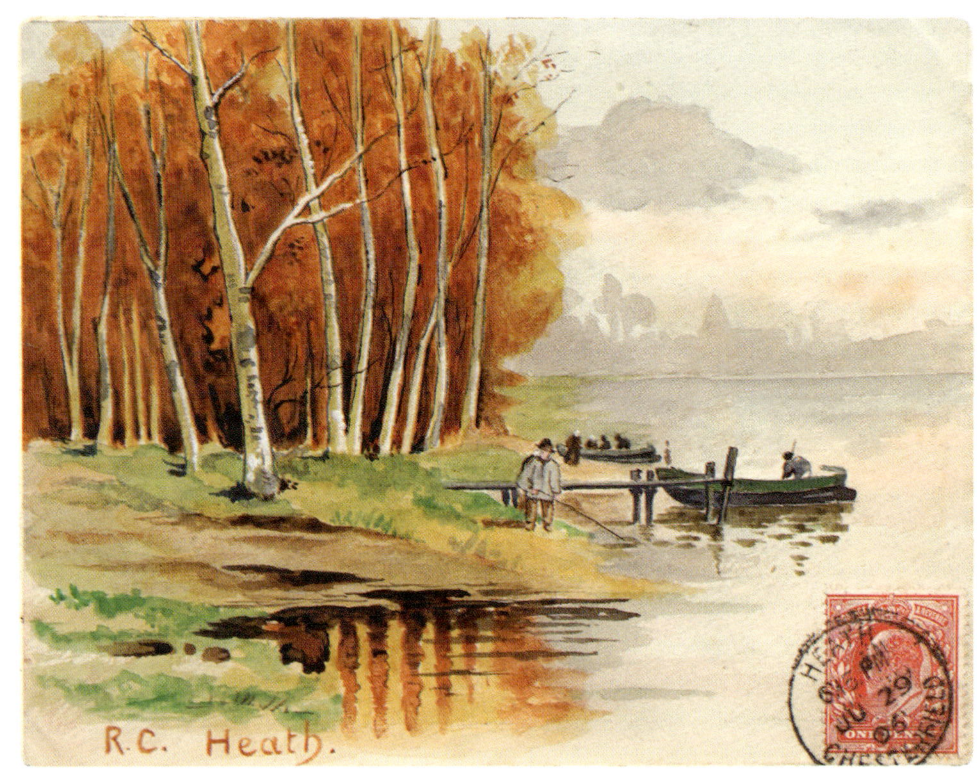

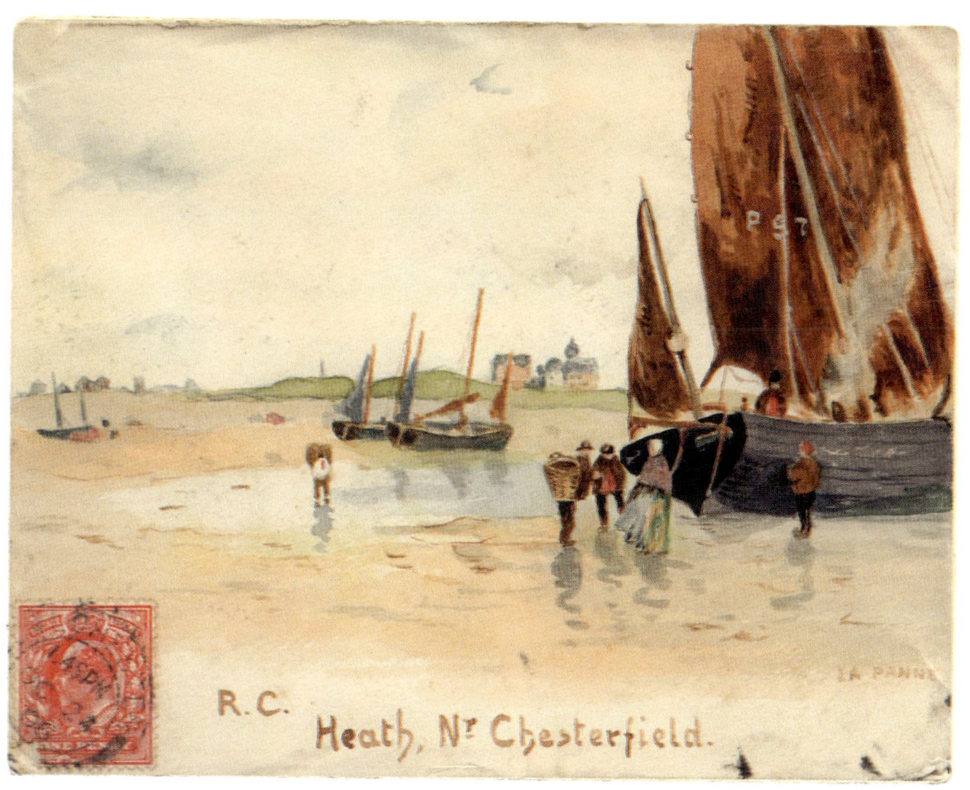
P 57
LA PANNE
R.C.
Heath, Nr Chesterfield.

Ruth,
England

In the Royal Naval School magazine, Miss Ruth Chignell describes a long hard day commencing at 6:15 am, bathing in cold water, no talking anywhere, breakfast of cocoa and bread and butter, walks around the grounds in all weathers plus all the lessons.

[Starting as] a boarder at the Royal Naval School, Ruth then took up a career in teaching, with her aunt Jemima as mentor.

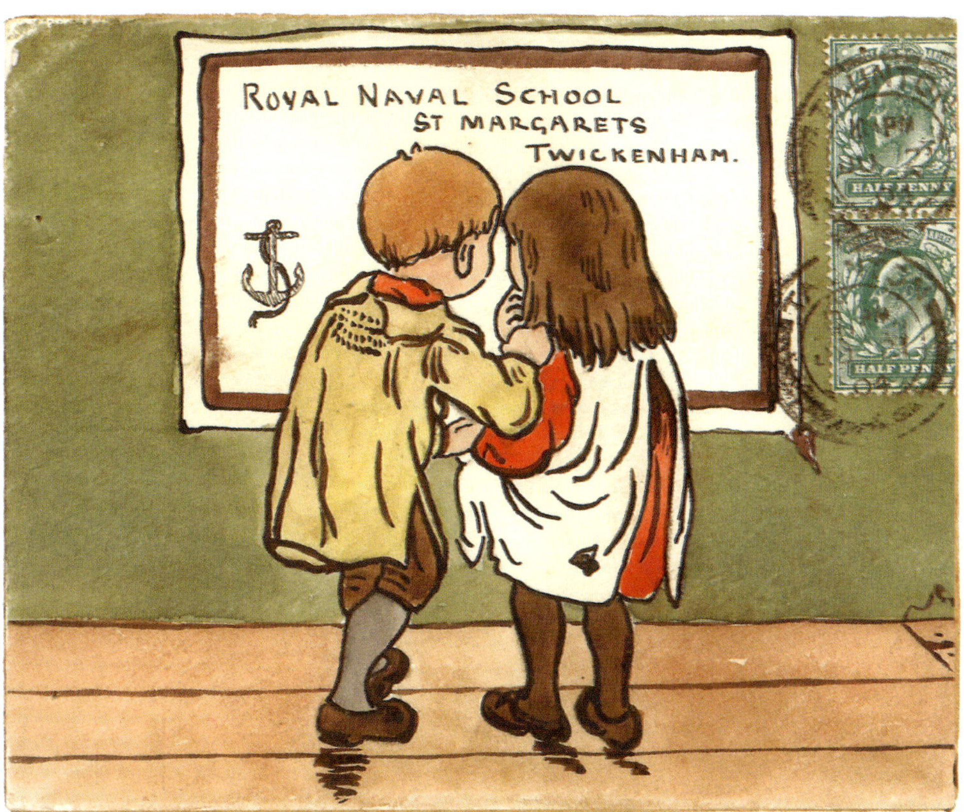

ENGLAND
Home Team, Ruth

Chichester
Bishop Otter College

Twickenham
Royal Naval School

Chesterfield
Heath Village School for Girls

Redcar, North Riding
Girls' Central School

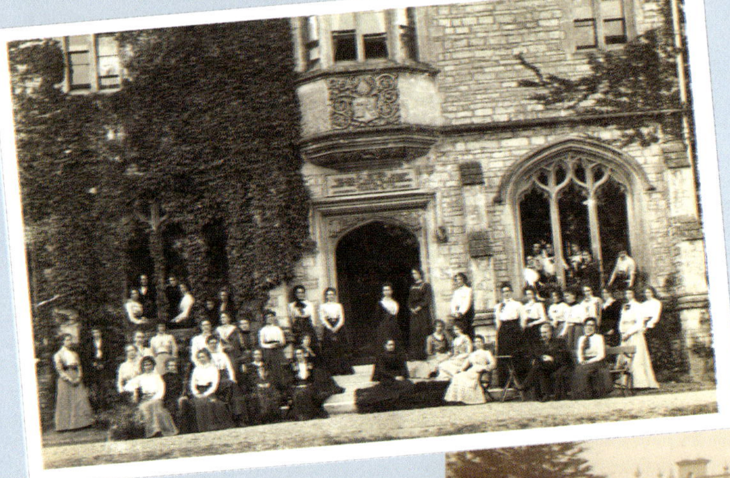

Ruth's initial training (1896-1899) was at Bishop Otter College (top) in Chichester, which in 1873 had become a training college for women as a result of a campaign to encourage the acceptance of women as teachers, Jemima having been an early student.

After several short-term positions Ruth joined the staff at Royal Naval School in 1902, her aunt still Lady Governess as she had been when Ruth was a boarder.

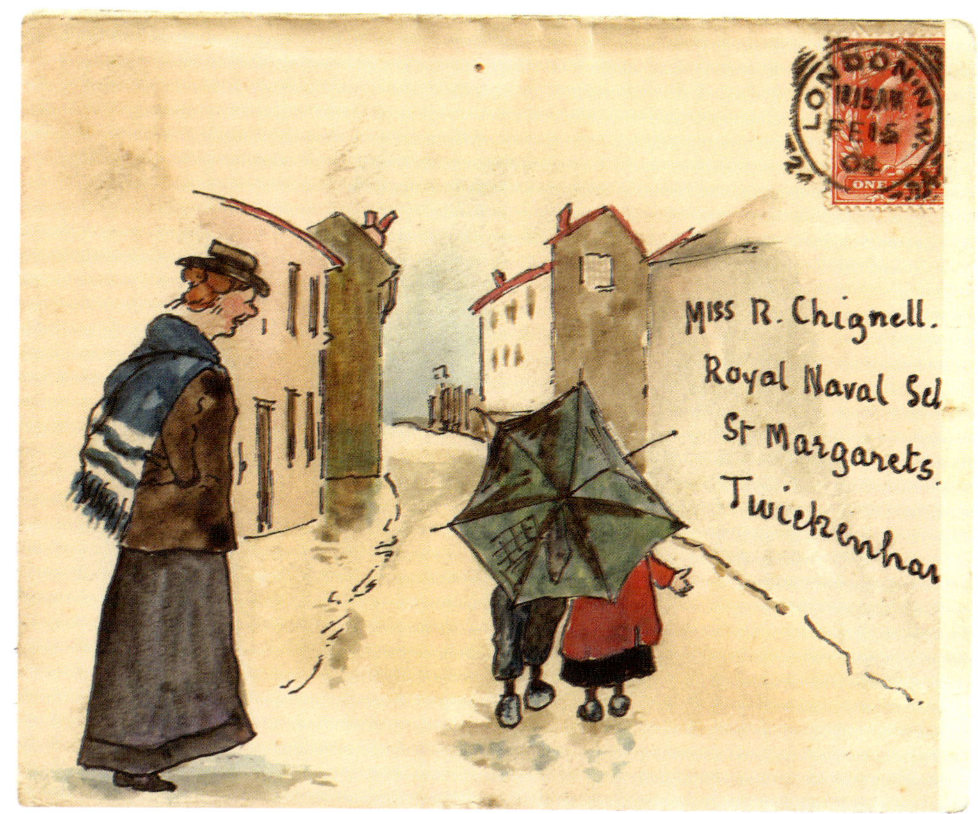

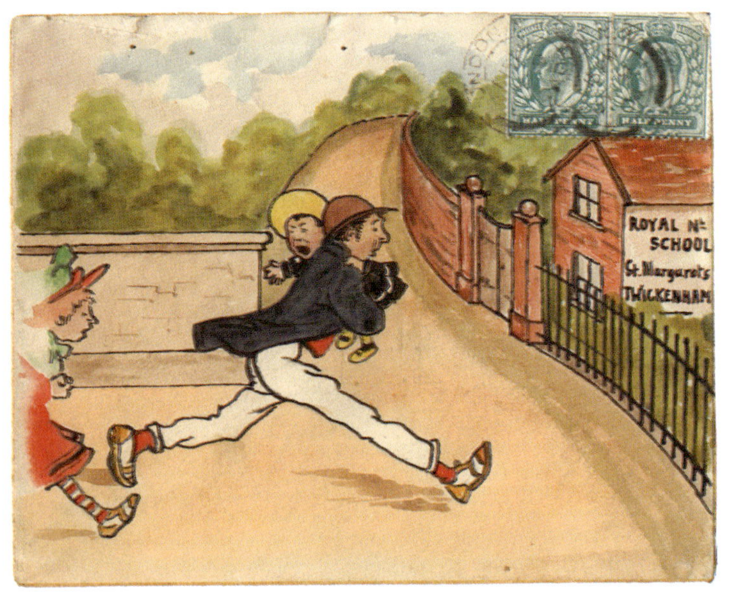
ROYAL N.
SCHOOL
St. Margarets
TWICKENHAM

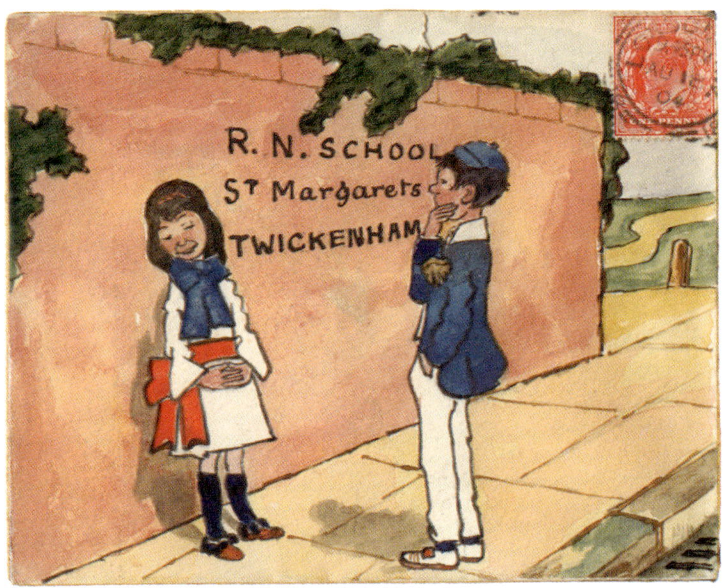
R. N. SCHOOL
St Margarets
TWICKENHAM

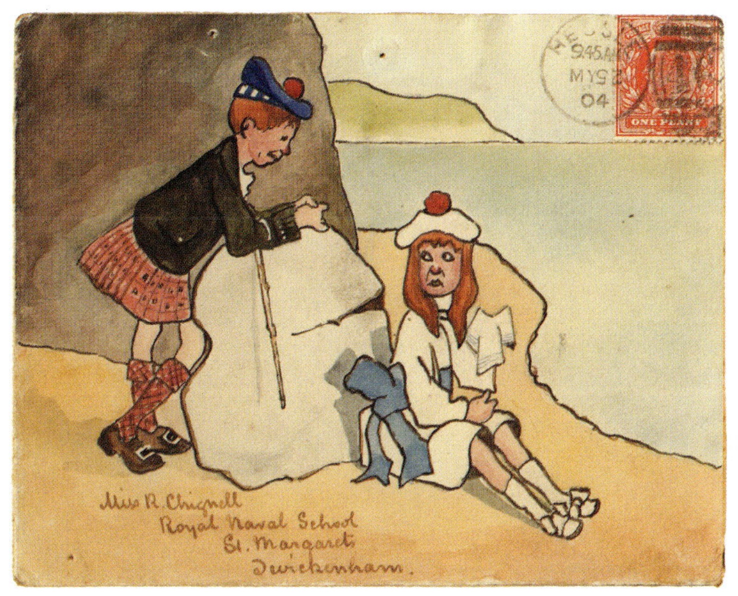
Miss R. Chignell
Royal Naval School
St. Margaret's
Twickenham.

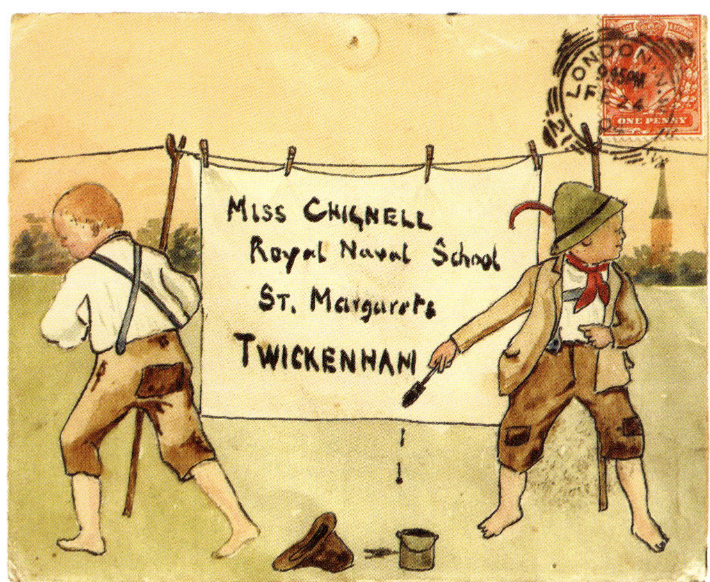
MISS CHIGNELL
Royal Naval School
ST. Margaret's
TWICKENHAM

In 1904 Ruth became headmistress of the village school for girls and infants at Heath near Chesterfield. She remained at Heath until 1907 when she returned to Chichester as Head Mistress of the Practising School at Bishop Otter College where she stayed until 1922 when she moved to Redcar in the North Riding of Yorkshire as headmistress of the Girls' Central School at South Bank.

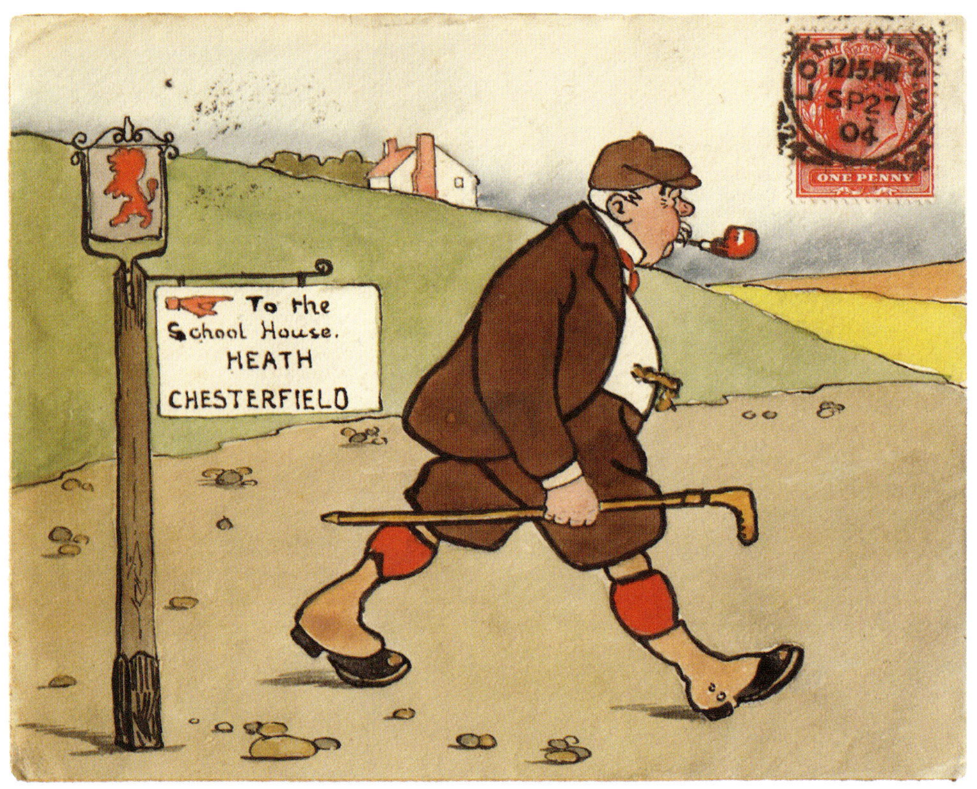

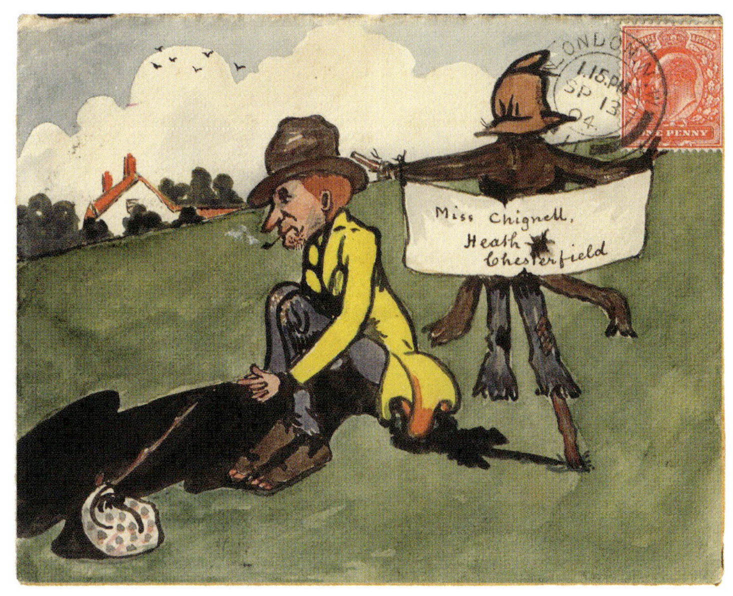
Miss Chignell,
Heath
Chesterfield

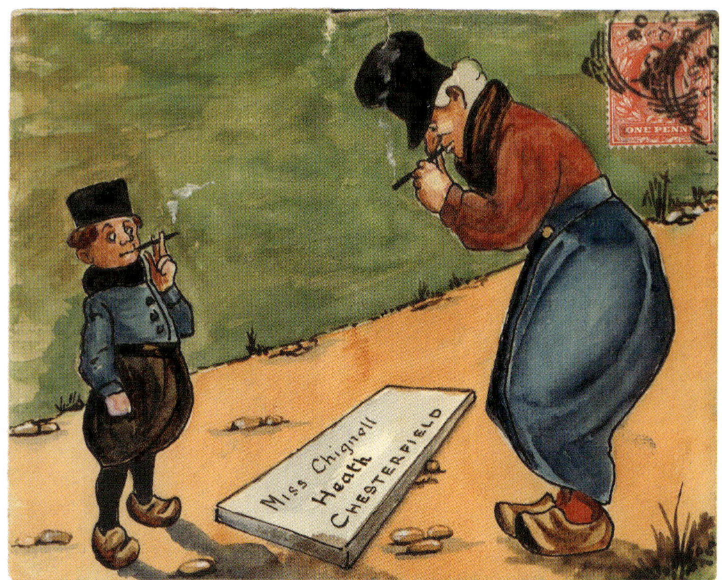
Miss Chignell
Heath
CHESTERFIELD

Ruth is long-worded. She will take up a whole page where a couple of lines would do. She is too strict and her grammar too correct. She writes like the school marm she is.

Phil writing to Isabel, 10 February 1929

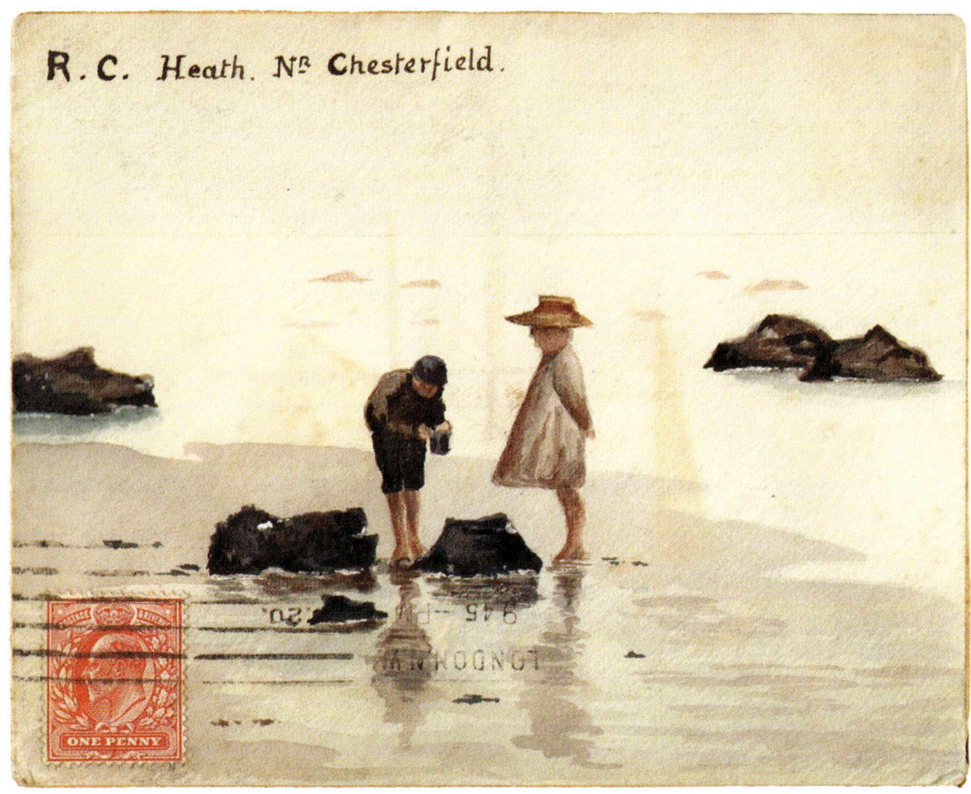

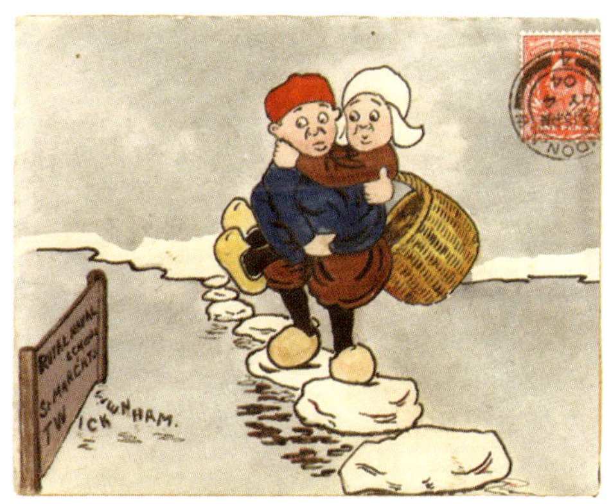
ROYAL NAVAL
SCHOOL
St MARGATS
TWICKENHAM.
N.B.

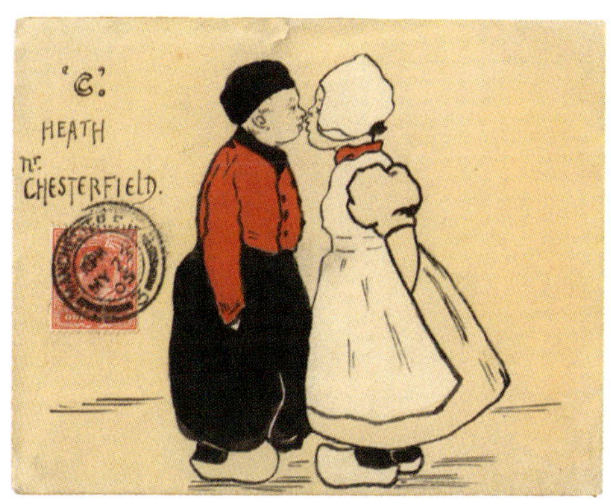
"C."
HEATH
Nr
CHESTERFIELD.

Madge,
England

ENGLAND
Home Team, Madge

New Barnet

Leominster
1905

I always say that Madge never had any encouragement to be clever at anything outside domestic work, but all the same old Madge just sits down and writes what is in her thoughts at the moment.

Humdrum things often enough, the curate came to tea or her friend Mrs J. has had her third baby. But there, Leominster is a hum-drum sort of a place and Madge just reflects that idea in her letters but all the same her letters are interesting.

Phil writing to Isabel on 10 February 1929

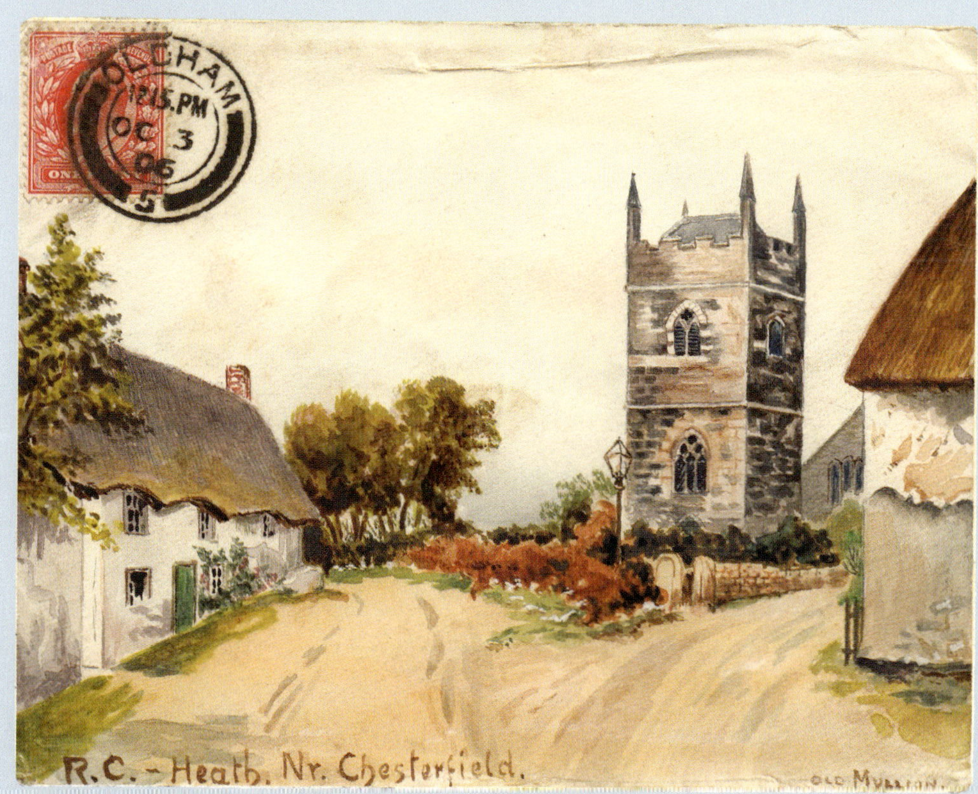

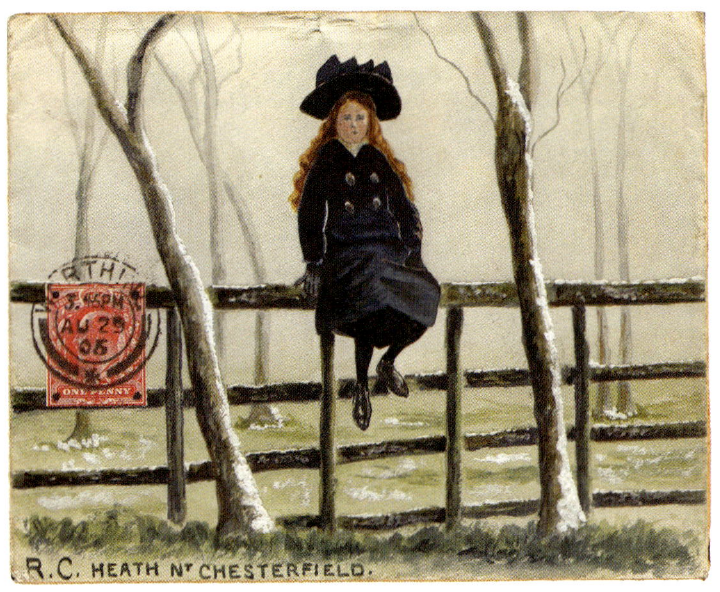

R.C. HEATH Nr CHESTERFIELD.

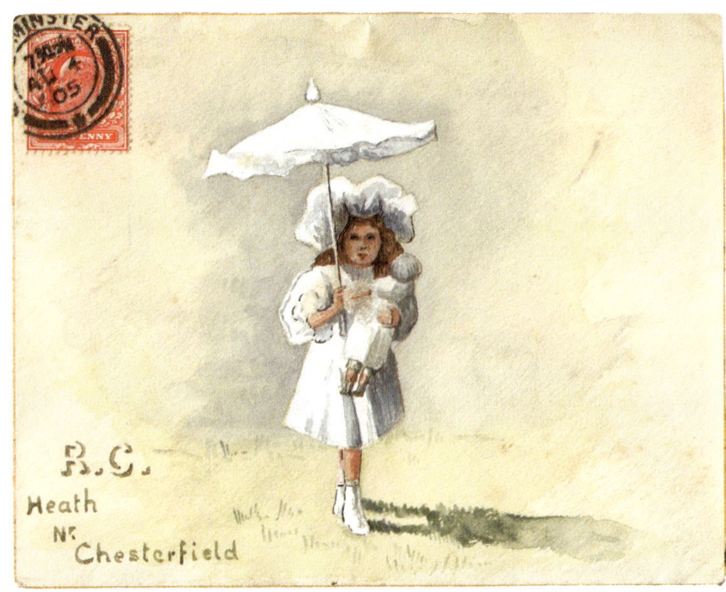

R.C.
Heath
Nr
Chesterfield

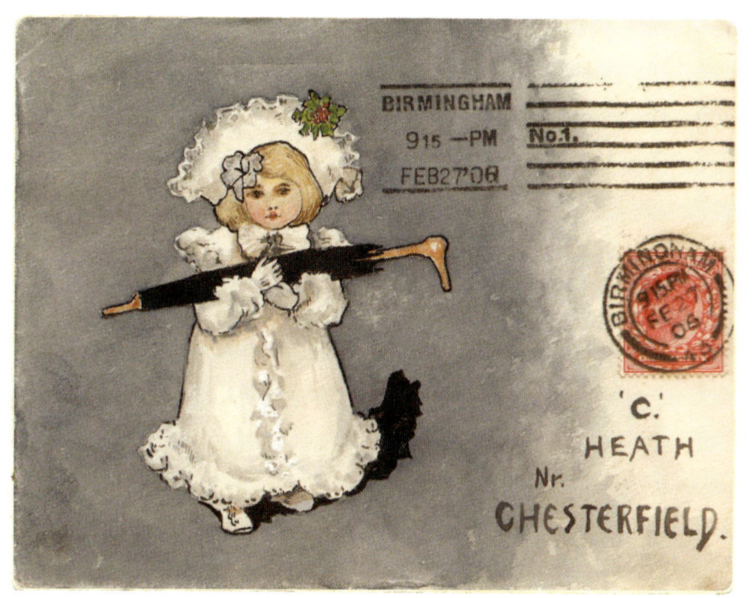
BIRMINGHAM
9.15 —PM   No.1.
FEB27'06
'C.'
HEATH
Nr.
CHESTERFIELD.

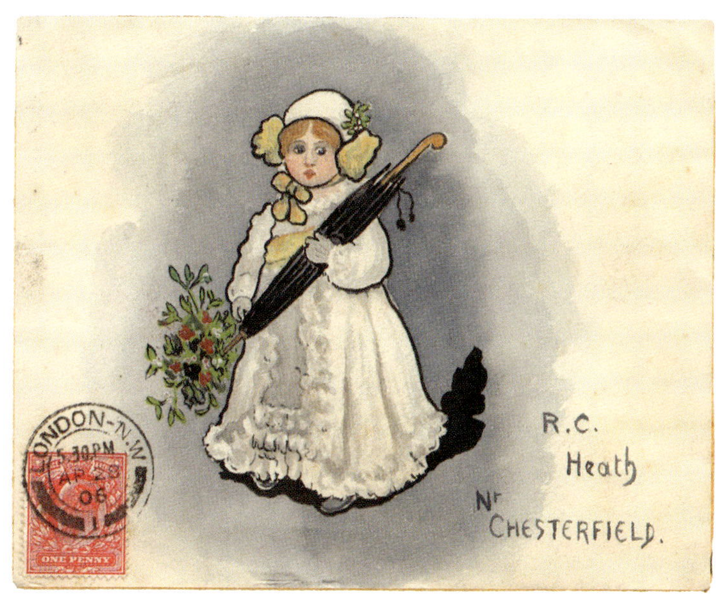
LONDON-N.W
ONE PENNY
R.C.
Heath
Nr
CHESTERFIELD.

There was a period during which
I was in many ways the favourite
choirboy, because my organist was
courting my sister and I was a very
useful intermediary for notes &c

*Norman was a choirboy when Herbert
Crimp was the Organist at Holy Trinity
Church, Barnet....*
*The ploy was successful and in 1897
Madge and Herbert were married.*

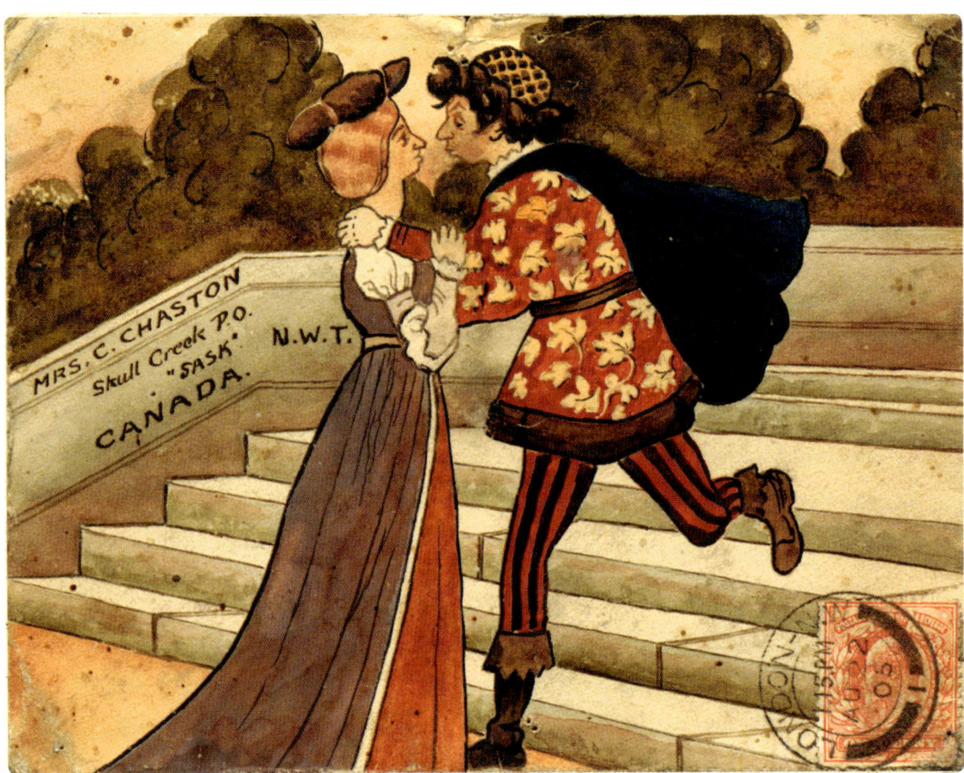

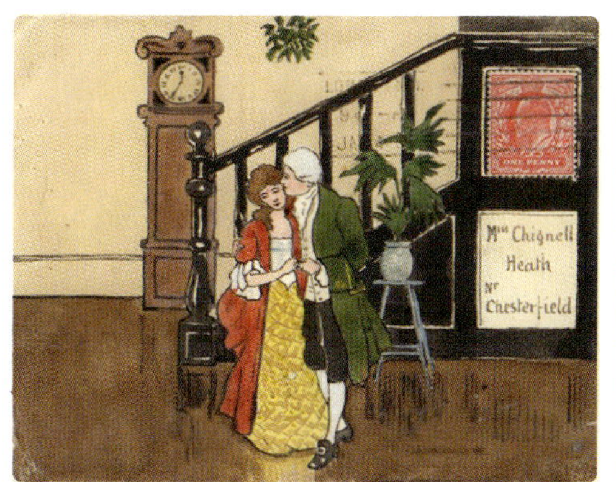
ONE PENNY
Mrs Chignell
Heath
Nr
Chesterfield

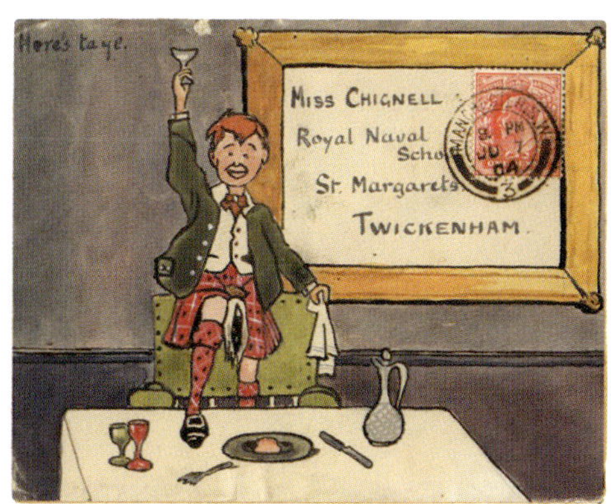
Here's taye.
MISS CHIGNELL
Royal Naval
Schol
St. Margarets
TWICKENHAM

In 1905 Madge and Herbert moved
to Leominster where Herbert
became the organist and choir
master at the Priory Church.

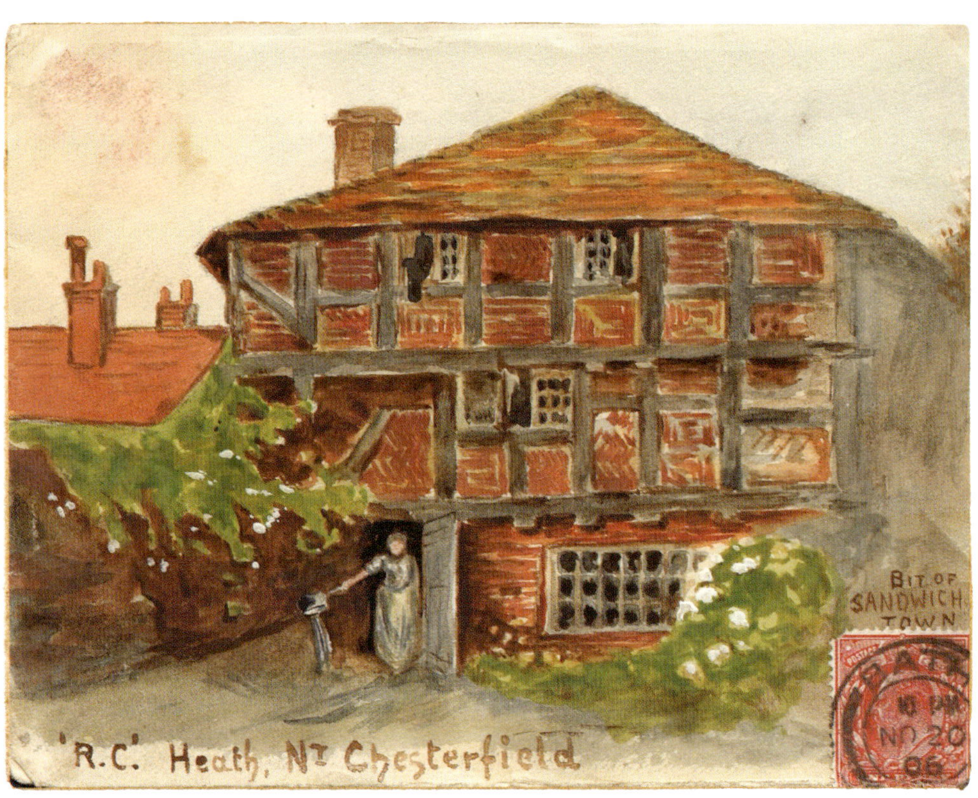

The earliest surviving envelope was sent to Madge after her marriage to Herbert Crimp.

This slighly later one was sent to Norman, known as FEU, while he was staying with Madge.

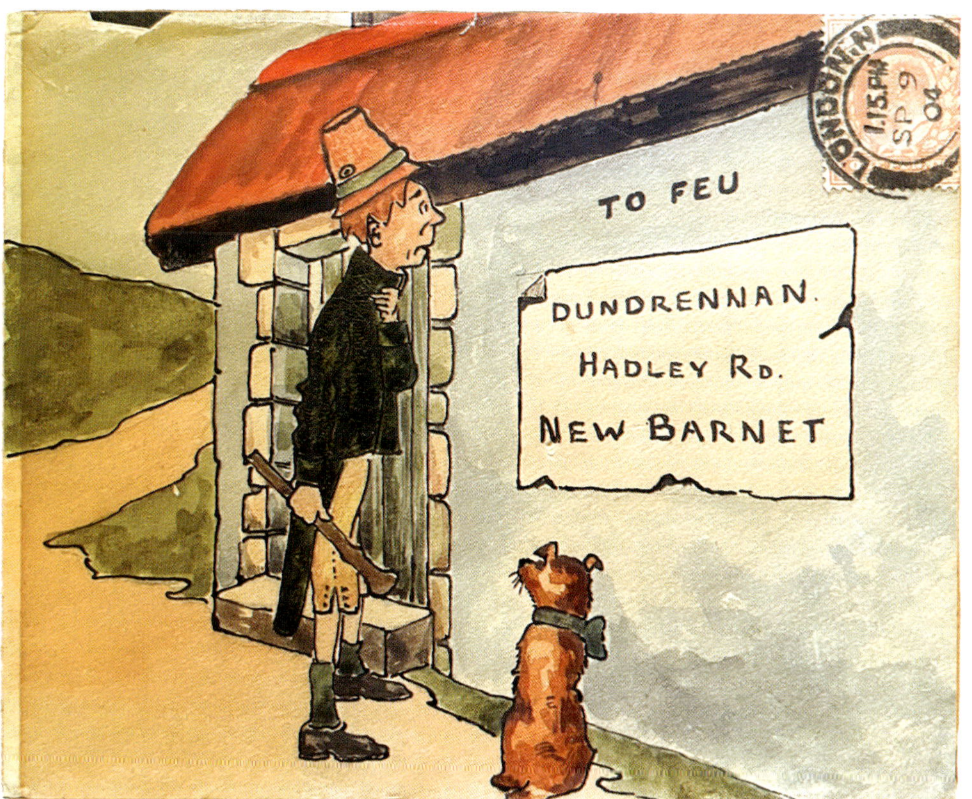

It was at Leominster Madge began her visitors book in 1908. Many of the entries came from her siblings who returned briefly from abroad.

In August 1909, shortly before he moved to his nearby 'Shobdon Retreat' Harry stayed with Madge, describing his 'good times and happy meetings' and attaching a watercolour drawing as well:

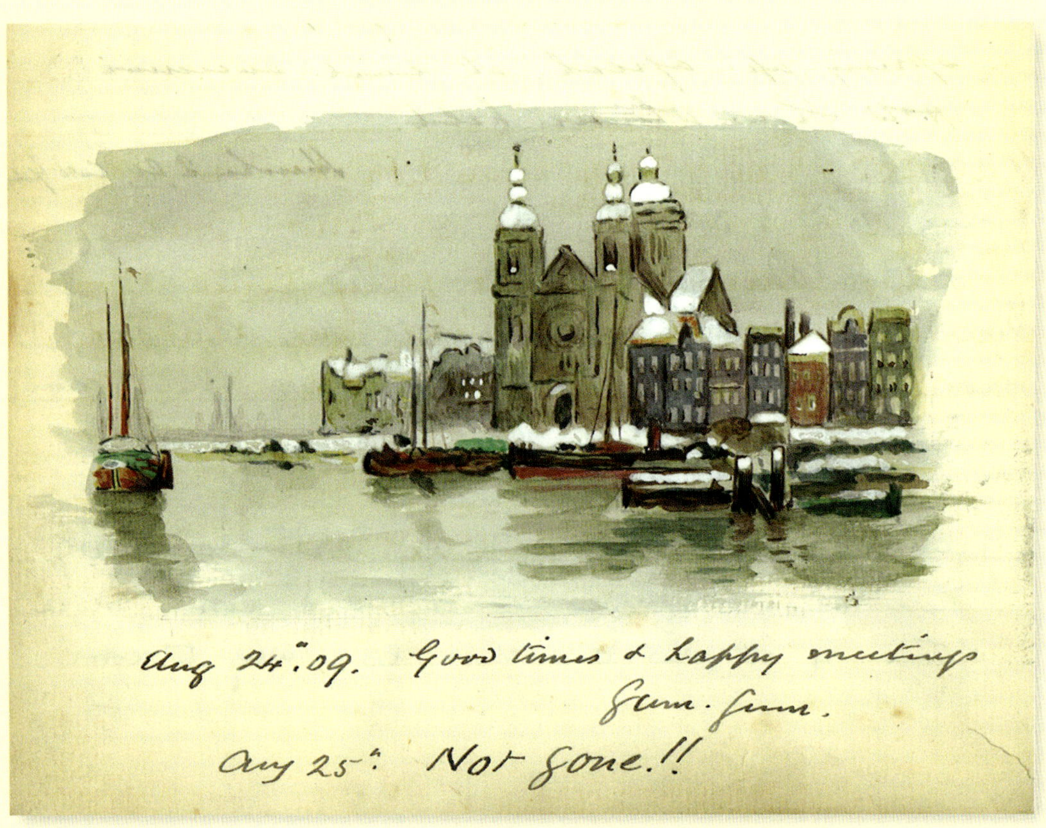

Madge's house was an important hub for the family. Here we have examples of the signatures of her siblings. Each year had a heading with a new date and this example is by Harry, known to the family as Gum Gum.

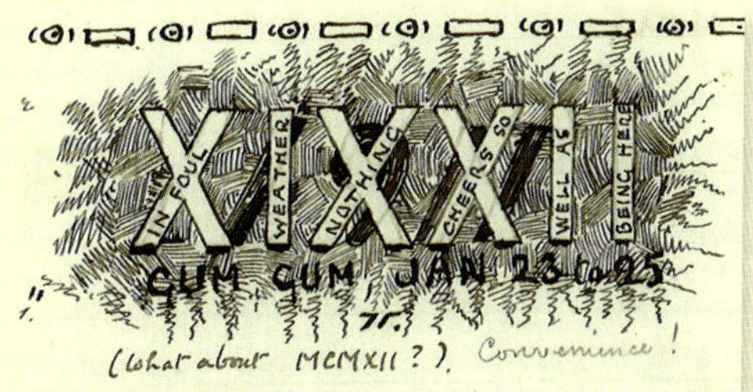

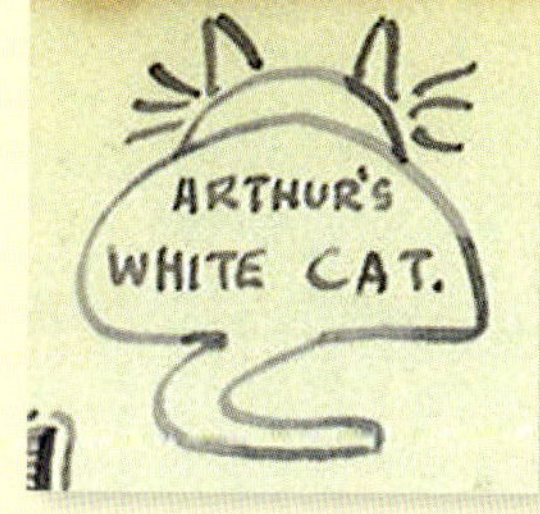

Eliza,
Harry's wife

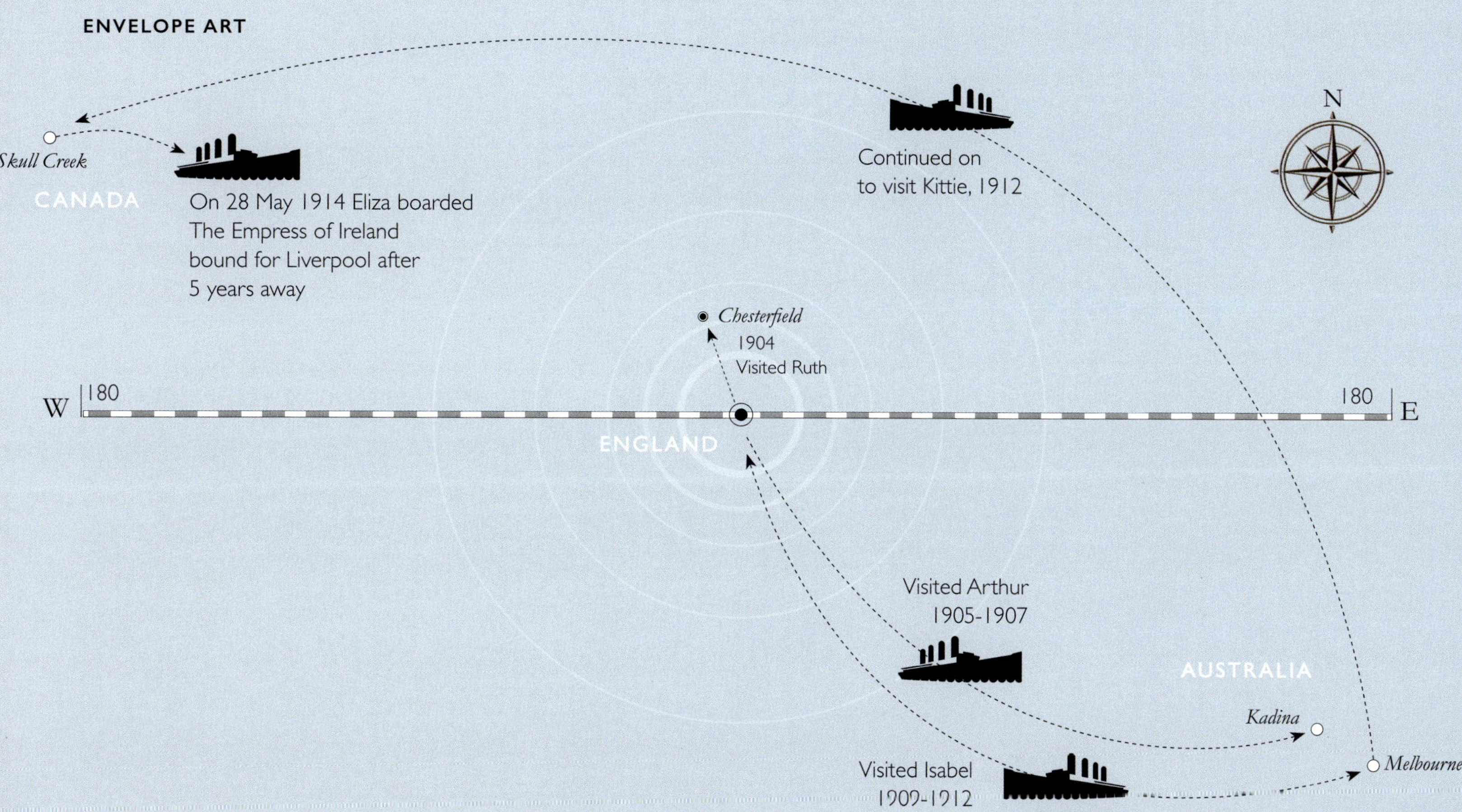
Skull Creek
CANADA
On 28 May 1914 Eliza boarded
The Empress of Ireland
bound for Liverpool after
5 years away
Continued on
to visit Kittie, 1912
N
Chesterfield
1904
Visited Ruth
W 180
180 E
ENGLAND
Visited Arthur
1905-1907
AUSTRALIA
Kadina
Melbourne
Visited Isabel
1909-1912

After the break-up both of her household and her marriage in 1899, Eliza soon began what would be a regular pattern for the rest of her life: staying for prolonged periods with her children and regularly helping out with grandchildren.

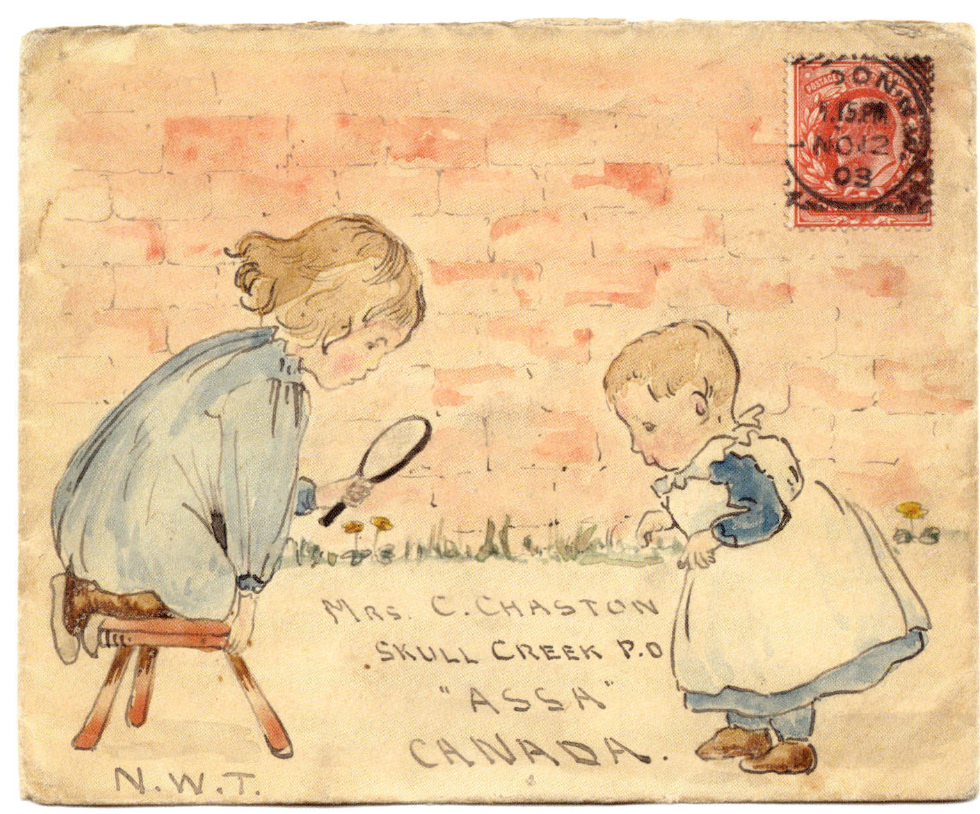

What was she coming to?
We in England often wondered. She and Father
were usually bickering when they were together and the fates (or design)
had separated them for so long that they had almost forgotten what it
meant to be in the same house. And here they were — both 70 or over — almost
compelled to live together in their old age, and in cirumstances that could
not fail to be difficult... There was just nothing for it but for them to live together
at Shobdon and we couldn't see how it was going to work.

Norman's diary She (mother) was to return home in the Empress of Ireland in May

The year 1914 is fixed in the memory
of all people alive in that year.
For me it was more than the year
of the outbreak of war. For in
May of that year Mother was due
to return to England after her
last round-the-world journey.

And then, tragically, the problem
(mother's return) was solved in a
way that none of us has anticipated.
For the *Empress of Ireland* was
rammed in the fog in the
St Lawrence River, and went
down in a few minutes.

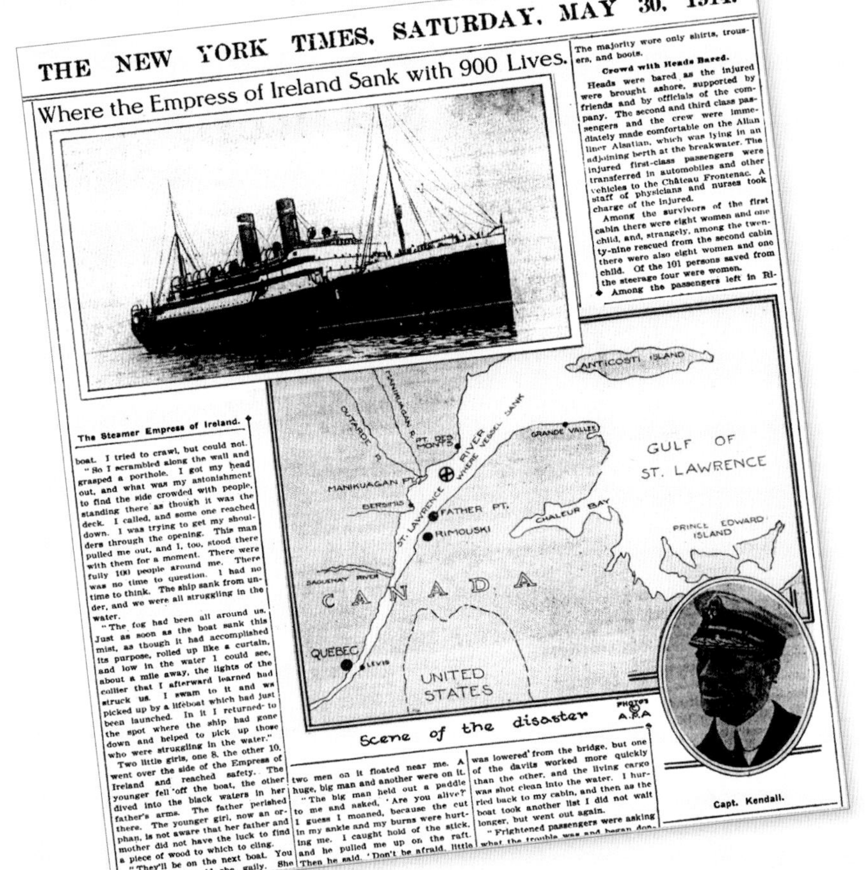

THE NEW YORK TIMES, SATURDAY, MAY 30, 1914.

Where the Empress of Ireland Sank with 900 Lives.

The Steamer Empress of Ireland.

boat. I tried to crawl, but could not.
"So I scrambled along the wall and grasped a porthole. I got my head out, and what was my astonishment to find the side crowded with people, standing there as though it was the deck. I called, and some one reached down. I was trying to get my shoulders through the opening. This man pulled me out, and I, too, stood there with them for a moment. There were fully 100 people around me. There was no time to question. I had no time to think. The ship sank from under, and we were all struggling in the water.

"The fog had been all around us. Just as soon as the boat sank this mist, as though it had accomplished its purpose, rolled up like a curtain, and low in the water I could see, about a mile away, the lights of the collier that I afterward learned had struck us. I swam to it and was picked up by a lifeboat which had just been launched. In it I returned to the spot where the ship had gone down and helped to pick up those who were struggling in the water."

Two little girls, one 8, the other 10, went over the side of the Empress of Ireland and reached safety. The younger fell off the boat, the other dived into the black waters in her father's arms. The father perished there. The younger girl, now an orphan, is not aware that her father and mother did not have the luck to find a piece of wood to which to cling.

"They'll be on the next boat. You wait and see," said she, gaily. She

The majority wore only shirts, trousers, and boots.

Crowd with Heads Bared.

Heads were bared as the injured were brought ashore, supported by friends and by officials of the company. The second and third class passengers and the crew were immediately made comfortable on the Allan liner Alsatian, which was lying in an adjoining berth at the breakwater. The injured first-class passengers were transferred in automobiles and other vehicles to the Château Frontenac. A staff of physicians and nurses took charge of the injured.

Among the survivors of the first cabin there were eight women and one child, and, strangely, among the twenty-nine rescued from the second cabin there were also eight women and one child. Of the 101 persons saved from the steerage four were women.

Among the passengers left in Ri-

Scene of the disaster

two men on it floated near me. A huge, big man and another were on it. "The big man held out a paddle to me and asked, 'Are you alive?' I guess I moaned, because the cut in my ankle and my burns were hurting me. I caught hold of the stick, and he pulled me up on the raft. Then he said, 'Don't be afraid, little

was lowered from the bridge, but one of the davits worked more quickly than the other, and the living cargo was shot clean into the water. I hurried back to my cabin, and then as the boat took another list I did not wait longer, but went out again.

"Frightened passengers were asking what the trouble was and began don-

Harry did not seem to regret the loss of his wife.

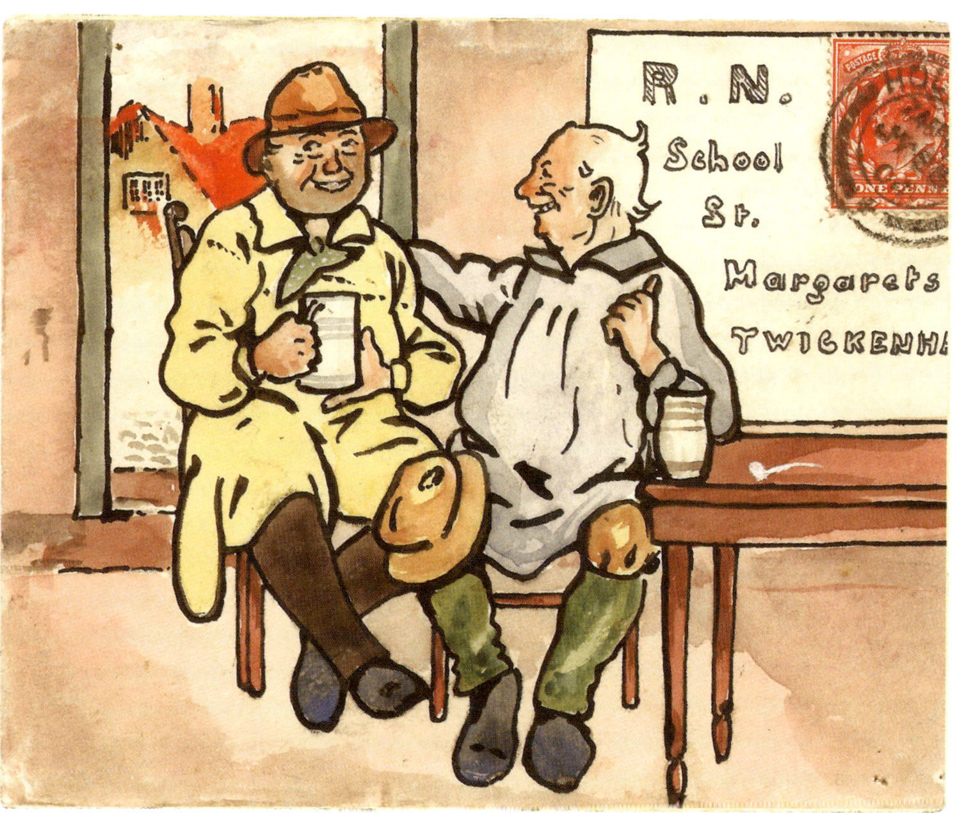

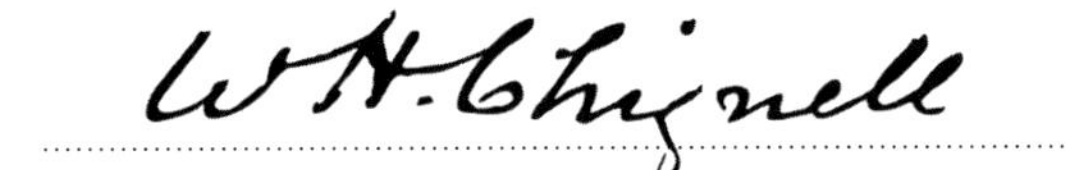

Drawings on the envelopes by W H Chignell

Text chosen by James P Carley.
James had a flat in the London Charterhouse between 2016 and 2020
and spent many a foggy evening walking through
the grounds hoping to meet his great-grandfather's ghost.

Designed by Katharine E Hutchison and with layout assistance by Karen Wilks.
Katharine's offices happen to be in the London Charterhouse.

ALMOST FORTY YEARS AGO Felicity Dodd visited my wife Ann M Hutchison and myself in the village of Haslingfield outside Cambridge when I was the Munby Fellow at the University. The grandaughter of Isabel Jamieson she brought from Australia large quantities of information on the Chignell family which she shared with us. Ever since then she regularly sent me and almost all of W H Chignell's great grandchildren new material as she wrote up histories of the family. This stream only dried up in 2023 when she approached her hundredth birthday.

Felicity is in a sense the inspiration for this book. Meanwhile, Guy Abel, one of Madge's great grandchildren, began gathering writings by Harry's children as well as envelopes. He has been generous in sharing his files with me and answering questions. I am very grateful to him. His cousin Richard Crimp transcribed Norman's diaries as did Philip's grandson Michael Geraghty his grandfather's accounts of his World Tour with the Sheffield Choir in 1911.

Rachel Koopmans, Department of History, York University, Toronto; James Willoughby, Librarian at Wichester College; and Fred Unwalla, Director of Publications, Pontifical Institute of Mediaeval Studies, Toronto, examined the manuscript on various occasions and made many useful suggestions.

In the mid-1980s I showed Pamela Wharton Blanpied, who had just published her book on *Dragons: the Modern Infestation* a selection of the envelopes and she wrote a short story, never published, envisaging the artist behind the drawings, a man about whom she knew nothing. She portrayed a curmudgeonly London busness man by the name of Leonard Medwen whose temperament was mellowed by his watercolours: '*The paintings remained uniformly mild. Tautness, control, craft, sensitivity, these informed both temper and paintings*'. It is a good evocation.

James P Carley

FURTHER READING AND ILLUSTRATION CREDITS

Online sources
The Postal Museum, Tolhurst Envelopes Parts 1 and 2.
The Postal Museum Blog: *Tolhurst Envelopes – The Postal Museum* and *Tolhurst Envelopes: Part 2 – The Postal Museum*
   (The Postal Museum, 2018)
The Postal Museum, The McLennan Mail Art.
The Postal Museum Blog: *The McLennan Mail Art – The Postal Museum* (The Postal Museum, 2016)
Ray Johnson: Home – Ray Johnson Estate
The Postal Museum, Postcards by Peter Liversidge
The Postal Museum Blog: *Postcards by Peter Liversidge – The Postal Museum* (The Postal Museum, 2021)

Publications
Duncan Campbell Smith, *Masters of the Post The Authorised History of the Royal Mail*, Penguin Books), London, 2011
Douglas N Muir, *Just Large Enough*, The Postal Museum, London, 2022

Illustration Credits
p.38 Family archive
p.42 Bridgeman Images
p.45 British Library, London
p. 72/73 Copyright Pitt Rivers Museum, University of Oxford
p. 94 top: University of Chichester, Special Collection; bottom: Alan Winter Postcard Collection
p.116 The New York Times (U.S. Newspaper 1914)